Growing Up Small

Joe Barbrie

CHARGER BOOKS

Copyright © 2017 by Joe Barbrie

All rights reserved. No part of this book may be reproduced or transmitted in any form without written permission from the publisher, except by reviewers who may quote brief excerpts in connection with a review.

If you purchased this book without a cover, you should be aware that it was an unauthorized sale. All books without a cover have been reported as "unsold and destroyed." As a result neither the author nor the publisher received payment for the sale of this "stripped book."

A special thanks to Margaret Carroll, my 4th grade teacher, who provided the old photographs.

Printed in the USA
ISBN 978-0-692-90245-5

CHARGER BOOKS
320 Camellia Ct
El Dorado Hills, CA 95762

Visit us at www.chargerbooks.com

Prologue

I was fortunate to grow up with fifty acres of pine trees, trails, and heavily wooded forest behind my house. We just called it *the Woods*. This is a place where we played, camped, ran with our dogs, and took our girlfriends to smooch. The woods were beautiful, mysterious, and, on a dark night, a little scary.

We paved footpaths, built tree houses, and made daring sled runs through the trees and rocks during the winter. There were ghosts and legends in the woods: the lost ice skater from Cranberry Pond, the old guy who died in a sod house, and the maniac skeleton drivers of the deserted old junk cars were just a few of the spirits haunting the woods.

I will visit Millville, Massachusetts a few more times before I pass on and go to that big ball field in the sky. I don't know when I'll go again, but when I do it will be like I never left more than forty years ago. One thing I am sure of, the meadow and the woods where my friends and I played will still be there. My old elementary school is now a historic building and the WWII Memorial Park endures. Some of our old haunts and hangouts may have been torn down or renovated, but spirits linger. There are a few of the old folks still around, a tribute to how the slow pace of life and low stress can help a soul be happy and live longer.

Welcome to what the world was like in my youth and how it was to grow up during the 1960s. I hope you enjoy my little stories of life in the easy lane, and I hope I stir a few old memories for you.

Blackstone River

CHAPTER 1

The Background

Setting the Stage

I grew up in a small town in Massachusetts during the 1960s. Millville, Massachusetts, first settled in 1662, was incorporated in 1916 and celebrated its Centennial in 2016. The town is rich in history and part of the Blackstone River Valley National Heritage Corridor. Some of my stories include our escapades in and around historical places like the Chestnut Street Meeting House and the old Blackstone Canal and locks.

During the first two decades of the twentieth century, Major League Baseball great, Gabby Hartnett, born in Woonsocket, Rhode Island, grew up in Millville. He played youth baseball in the Blackstone Valley League before playing for the Chicago Cubs in 1922. The house where Gabby lived during his time in Millville was located only a few streets down from where I grew up and I got to know an old man who actually knew Gabby and had, what appeared to me as a young boy, a roomful of baseball nostalgia.

I remember visiting the old man and listening to him talk about old-time baseball. Sometimes he would show us his old baseball stuff that included an assortment of vintage baseball bats, balls, hats, and uniforms. I remember he also had lots of old yellowed newspapers. I don't know what ever happened to the old man. I guess in 1965 no one was too excited about this stuff, yet today it would be worth a fortune. Although Gabby died in 1972, he certainly left his mark on the town, there even being a sign in town with the inscription Charles L. "Gabby" Hartnett Memorial Highway.

As small towns go, Millville was an interesting place with history, a famous person or two, and enough cast of characters and events to, well, write a book about.

During my time living in Millville there were families with roots from across Europe. I was exposed to a unique blend of heritage, family traditions, and food. Many of the people I remember were unique because of where their roots were seeded. Maybe it was the food I remembered (or sometimes wanted to forget), the strange languages some of the grandparents still spoke, or just a custom from the old country. In any case, for me it was a multicultural learning experience and I consider myself fortunate.

Every small town has its history, legends, and memorable events. Sometimes small towns like Millville make for interesting storylines due to the cast of characters and tales that go along with those people. My life back then was simple compared to those of city kids or people from the upper classes of society. Millville was a blue-collar town to be sure. There weren't too many aristocrats walking around, as I recall.

But in present context, my time there would have made for a good reality television show. People might have gotten a big kick out of following my buddies and me around each day. Being part of our daily mayhem would be a lot more interesting and funnier than what is on television today.

My memories of this special little place are like a window that opens to let in fresh air and lets me think about a time long ago. Some memories are not so great, but most make me wish I could revisit them and play them out all over again. You can't go back, not in time anyway. But you can revisit old memories, places, and even a few old friends. Do it while you still can or they will be lost forever.

So, that sets the stage for what I hope is an interesting glimpse into what life was like for a kid growing up in a small, close-knit New England town back in the 1960s. *Sherman, to the WABAC machine!*

Let's Start Here

Everyone has childhood memories. We've all had special moments, high points, low points, joy and heartbreak. As we got older, those memories fade and sometimes we just wish things would've turned out better. While writing these stories, reviewing and editing the manuscript, I laughed a lot and sometimes cried. Each review stirred a new memory or brought a new tear to my eye.

Some people are honest with themselves, recalling things as they were. Others embellish a little here or bend a fact there, needing things to appear larger and more important than they were. I'm sure we have all stretched the truth a bit about past romances, sports accomplishments, and events we were part of. My high school baseball batting average goes up with each passing year, for one. And when I relive old baseball stories, I singlehandedly won more games than ever. I also drove the coolest car in town and dated the prettiest girl. *Right!*

Many recall their younger days with a smile, some with mixed feelings. But one thing I'm sure of, we all remember the lessons we learned, especially the hard ones. Sometimes you wish your stories had ended differently. Everyone wants to hit the big shot, catch the game-winning touchdown pass, and walk away with the prettiest girl. But alas, for most people, those things simply did not happen. I'm content to remember most of these events as they happened and live happily ever after. That's exactly what I'm doing.

So be warned, nostalgia will run high, and even though it's harder to raise an eyebrow these days, I'm certain folks of all ages will appreciate this look back into time. It was a time when *real-time* wasn't a term that meant instant access, and a time when there were no cell phones to take photos of us doing stupid things to immediately be posted on social media. It was a time we did what we wanted to do without fear of political correctness or worldwide humiliation within minutes.

I think kids these days are trapped in behavior models that hinder their imagination. This deprives them of the opportunity to explore the spontaneous capacity within them. Ask any ten- or twelve-year-old kid today to tell you funny stories about his or her friends or family. Odds are there won't be much in the memory banks. Parents are too concerned about raising their children in this perfect little Utopia where everybody wins, no one loses, and everybody gets a corner office. That's not how the real world works, my friends.

I'm afraid we are raising a generation of youngsters that don't even know how to make eye contact anymore. Thank goodness for grandparents. We may be the last of a breed with common sense for preparing the younger generation for what lies ahead for them. This is a major difference from the 1960s and today. Sorry, I digress. I couldn't help taking a few shots at today's parenting.

I wish I could remember all of the interesting people I grew up with and more of the crazy things we did. Maybe you can fill in some of the spaces for yourself. If you are around my age, you will likely find similarities to your own youth. I clearly remember people who had a positive impact on me. On the other hand, there were also some I would like to forget but cannot.

I guess you could call some of these people oddballs, kooks, or just a little strange. Others were just normal folks who I recall fondly with a smile. There are a few special people who left a lasting impression, and their faces are etched in my mind, looking just as they did in 1965. As I write this, I am sixty-two years old, and it's been forty years since I've seen most of them. Still, I have great memories of many individuals who were kind, caring people who helped me on more than one occasion. Some were there for me at important stages in my life. And others just helped me out of a jam or cut me some slack when I needed it most. A special teacher, a great coach, and even an older guy I looked up to were some of my special people.

I believe certain people come into your life for a purpose and leave their personal impression on your mind and soul. We learn from them while providing them a garden of yet-to-be-cultivated young saplings yearning for guidance, knowledge, or just a friend. The good ones try to teach us what to do and what not to do, what to say and what not to say. They teach us how to win and how to lose. They help us to try to be a good person. Learning right from wrong is always a challenge, but we meet it head on and learn life lessons regardless of whether we make the right decisions.

Ours was a generation of hard workers. We kept things simple and guarded our individual privacy. We did not want to attract attention to ourselves and especially to what we were doing every single minute of the day. By comparison, people today—the young and the old—now seem to have a never-ending thirst for attention. I'm coining this acronym—DSAG—which to me stands for Desperately Seeking Attention Generation. (Maybe I'll make t-shirts one day and sell them on the Internet.) This lust for constant attention is satisfied by social media—some of it *is* good, but it can also be bad. I just imagine if someone had posted the crazy things my friends and I did while growing up. We would not have had half as much fun, that's for sure.

These are my stories of a time gone by with friends past and present. Some of the stories include family members and may upset a few relatives. Who cares? It's all true and based on the experiences of a young boy during an age of innocence. Well, maybe not so innocent. There is plenty of guilt to spread around and I was always a subject of investigation.

Many of my stories are unique and they did happen. After reading these tales, you will agree one can't make this stuff up. Having comedy, misfortune, and innocence occur at just the right time creates a priceless timepiece.

Just to let you know, most of the names have been changed to protect the guilty. And there were plenty of those guys.

The Roaring Sixties

Although politically turbulent, the 1960s was a great time to grow up, at least for me. The world was coming alive and I was eager to take in as much as I could. I'm a Baby Boomer, and I can say there certainly was a lot of booming going on back then. There were enough political and historical events in the 1960s to fill a lifetime. Many of those events shaped our country by changing attitudes and creating lasting opinions for generations to come. Throw in the escapades of my friends and I, and you have the makings of what I hope is an enjoyable tale from a bygone era.

Like most kids my age, I liked music, sports, and having fun.

Most of us had a record player and we listened to our favorite songs on 45s. No, these are not weapons. A 45 was a small round plastic disc on which a fine needle was lowered to its surface and produced sounds through a speaker (I don't know any other way to explain it to today's kids).

Anyway, I was ten years old in 1964 when The Beatles arrived in New York City. No one around my age has ever forgotten this historic musical event. This was big news and the beginning of what was called the *British Invasion*. A new wave of rock and roll music was introduced from England and our parents were not too keen on it, especially our dads.

These English bands with names like The Beatles, Rolling Stones, The Turtles, Herman's Hermits, and many others to follow created a wave of music that would forever change the way we listened, danced, and looked at rock and roll. With them they brought a sound and style that drove the U.S. girls crazy. Young girls everywhere were screaming, crying, and even fainting at the sight of these guys. They had funny haircuts, strange accents, and dressed in skinny suits and other weird clothes.

You know something? No girl ever fainted when they saw us no matter how good we played the guitar or what kind of clothes we wore. They usually made a sour face, stuck their tongue out at us, and ran as far away as they could.

I thought The Beatles looked weird with their stupid hair, skinny suits, and ties. After a while, though, everybody started to like the music more and more, and guys started to let their hair grow longer. Hey, it was working for The Beatles, so what the heck.

Many teenage boys got their hair cut just like the Beatles, but not all. There were still a few poor guys whose dads had been drill sergeants in the Marines, tough cops, or something like that. Those guys had a crew cut until, much to their father's dismay, they too changed their look, imitating the British invaders.

We were all hoping that if we looked and acted like them, our chances with the girls would improve. The mere possibility of fainting females was just too much to pass up. Sadly, the girls did not faint and the advances of us imposters went unnoticed. Maybe it was because The Beatles had a lot of money, fame, and had been on *The Ed Sullivan Show*. None of my friends or I had much money and we sure never did make it to *The Ed Sullivan Show*.

Although the girls did come around to liking us a little better with our new haircuts, our dads still did not like The Beatles, the new hair, or that crazy "yeah, yeah, yeah" music. Many of these guys were veterans from World War II and Korea and they were still sporting buzz cuts or real man haircuts as they referred to them. They were not happy with their son's new hair, clothes, or the music. But, even with our new Beatle hairstyle, the girls did not scream, sigh, or faint at the sight of us. What was it those guys from England had that we didn't?

Another huge event came in December of 1968 with Apollo 8. It was the first manned spacecraft to leave earth's atmosphere and reach the moon's orbit and safely return to earth. We watched, glued to our TVs, as three guys entered a tiny capsule at the top of a giant rocket and were blasted off into space. And just seven months later, Apollo 11 launched and Neil Armstrong and Buzz Aldrin were the first to walk on the surface of the moon. The moon!

How cool was this stuff! Screw the sissy Beatles, this made us dream of being famous astronauts and just maybe the type of real guy that girls might scream and faint over. But once again, that destiny was not to be ours. None of us turned out to be astronaut material. Reluctantly, we had to set our sights on something a little more reasonable. The fainting ladies would have to wait for a while. I'm still waiting although my wife faints sometimes, but I think that's maybe because I did something stupid. Come to think of it, she faints a lot.

The late sixties also brought in an era of even longer hair for the guys, jean jackets, bell-bottom pants, and peace-sign neck chains. I guess some of us were even hippies. It was a good time to be a teenage guy, though. All the girls wore mini-skirts, hip huggers, hot pants, and halter tops. Every girl looked so cute back then and we were treated to an endless parade of skin each day. It was too much of a good thing. Much to our chagrin, girls soon started wearing too much clothing, as the unthinkable Granny Dress era was around the corner.

My generation hated the Vietnam War while our parent's generation hated the hippies who were protesting the war. It was easy to get a rise out of the establishment and there was always plenty to complain about. But it was those hippies protesting the war (remember "Hey, Hey LBJ, how many kids did you kill today") influenced President Lyndon Baines Johnson to not seek re-election and eventually help put an end to it.

We were a little too young to fully understand the assassinations of President John F. Kennedy (JFK), Martin Luther King, and Bobby Kennedy, but we saw how much people cared about them. We tried to understand what they stood for and why it mattered so much.

I wish I had understood more about the Civil Rights Movement and the plight of African Americans during this time. There were very few black families in town but I do remember the vulgar names they had been called and how they were treated back then. Even in a small town in Massachusetts full of "good Christians," prejudice and ignorance was around every corner.

The Cold War was something we heard about on the news quite often. But seriously, as ten-year-old kids, we didn't really care if a war was hot, cold, or lukewarm. We could not comprehend the fact that there were thousands of nuclear missiles pointed at the enemy and we were ready to annihilate each other at the mere push of a few buttons.

But why should we be scared or have been concerned? We were told that there was nothing to fear. Our teachers and elders told us we were more than prepared for any attack. If we were at school during an attack, all we had to do was duck under our wooden desk. The old brick school building built in 1927 and our sturdy wooden desks would surely protect us from any nuclear fireball that came our way.

When you're a little kid you think differently and you believe everything the teacher and your parents tell you. We didn't even want to understand what was going on around us. We expected forever protection and assurance that everything would be all right in the world. Well, forever is long time and the idea of living in a never-ending safe-haven was indeed a dream. That dream was our reality, however, and for a few short years, it was nice to be just an innocent little kid. Thinking back, we were like small flakes of snow during a snowstorm. And that snowstorm was forming into a blizzard right around the corner. It was called life.

It's plain to see that times were a lot different when I was a young boy. I believe most young people today will never experience what my friends and I took for granted, just another ordinary day of running around, jumping out of trees, riding bikes, and scraping knees—pretty much a daily ritual.

Most of time our days were predictable and uneventful. Nothing very strange ever happened and each day was a snapshot of the day before with few minor changes. Predictability bred security and we found comfort in that. We could count on the same thing day in and day out, and if something out of the ordinary did happen, it was an event, one that could consume a whole day of new adventures and stories for me to tell.

So we learned life's lessons on the fly and created memories while living in one of the most interesting periods of our time. We were oblivious to the dangers in the world because we felt safe in our small town, isolated from the worries of the world. We knew that in some other countries there were little kids without enough food to eat, living in horrible conditions, and some were in the middle of wars. But here in our little place, our sanctuary of Americana, we did not have to think or worry about of the plight of millions around the world. It wasn't that we didn't care, more that we were just not personally connected to the bad things going on around the world. We were kids during a time of innocence on a theme park ride called rite of passage.

To be honest, I'm glad we lived in an era where we did not have smartphones, the Internet, and TV blasting the non-stop opinions of talking head crackpots. Censorship was kind of neat back then even if it was a little too controlling. But it was good enough for us kids and kept us away from most of the dirt of today's world. It was great to be a kid back then. Parents, relatives, and friends were always around to help us, but not coddle us. Life in 1965 may have been less complicated, but I wager it was more fun and a lot more interesting than being a kid today.

World War II Memorial Park

Chapter 2

Field of Dreams

The Meadow

During summer vacation, we were on our own almost every day. We didn't need to know nor did we care what was going on in the world. School was out and all we cared about was when the next baseball game down at *the Meadow* would start. The Meadow was a magical place. Although it was just a little league field next to a big old textile factory, it was our "field of dreams."

Back in the 1930s, the field was larger and some serious old time baseball was played there. An old Independent League semi-pro team played baseball there and from time to time, and even some professional players of the time showed up.

As I mentioned previously, Millville was home to major league ballplayer Gabby Hartnett, a Hall of Fame catcher from the 1920s who played for the Chicago Cubs. We heard the stories about Gabby and some of his friends having played ball down at the Meadow, the very place where we played.

As I also mentioned, my pals and I knew this old man who lived on the same street as Gabby had and was a big baseball fan. He had this one area in a room of his house where he kept all kinds of baseball memorabilia. It was full of cool stuff, including all kinds of old wooden baseball bats, balls, jerseys, and an assortment of baseball memorabilia.

This one day, we were playing baseball down at the Meadow and we were

Gabby Hartnett

down to our last good baseball. By then, the ball was getting pretty beat up, the lacings were loosening, and there was a rip in the ball; even the dog had gotten to it a few times. The ball was beginning to come unsewn and unravel more and more with each smack of the bat. Finally, one kid hit it so hard it unravels all the way to the string and small rubber core that makes up the inside every baseball. Game over. It was time for everyone to go home and beg our parents to buy us a new ball.

It was still early in the afternoon and I had an idea. I remembered seeing all those baseballs in the old man's house and I thought perhaps I could do a few good chores for him in exchange for a good baseball or two. So I promised to wash and wax his 1958 Chevrolet Bel-Air sedan once a month for the summer—and we had a deal.

The Chevy was silver blue and only had about 300 miles on it. The old guy had bought it new in 1958 and only drove it the

4 miles to and from church every Sunday along with a few short trips to the market. I continued to wash and wax this car up until around 1972 when I left town. I later heard he had left the car to some relative who had never come to seen him. I had cleaned that car for many years and secretly hoped that someday he would leave it to me. But family comes first and I lost out on a real classic.

However, I did get to choose a couple of baseballs that day. Now, the old guy could not see very well and was hard of hearing, too. He told me to pick out two baseballs in exchange for the work I promised, so I picked the two balls that looked the best and walked out the door with them. They were not brand new, but still in good ball-playing condition. They had ink writing on them and the names of a couple of guys I did not know or even care about.

Who cared about a ball with the name of some guy named Dizzy scribbled on it, or another with the name Cool Bubbel. Cool Bubbel, who the heck was this guy? Never heard of him. Turns out, Dizzy was the pitcher Dizzy Dean, a famous major league player and the last National League pitcher to win 30 games! Cool Bubbel was Carl Hubbell, the same guy who in the 1934 All Star game struck out Babe Ruth, Lou Gehrig, Jimmie Foxx, Al Simmons, and Joe Cronin in succession, setting a long-standing all-star game record for consecutive strikeouts during the All-Star game.

So, in our innocence we used these historic, now invaluable balls to play our meaningless baseball game. The sun was out, it was nice and warm, and we had baseballs. That was all that mattered to us. As we played, the names on the balls started to wear off and fade into the cowhide leather, never to be seen again. We scuffed them up, spit on them, threw them in the dirt, and bashed them the rest of that afternoon with our wooden bats.

We used them to what is ultimately the fate of all well-used baseballs as they go to their fate in the mouths of our dogs chewing on the ripped leather, string, and rubber core until there was nothing left. With the final stitching coming undone and the balls unravelling, we said farewell to Dizzy Dean and Carl Hubbell. We had fun doing it and I'm certain that Dizzy and Carl had a big smile on their face watching down on us kids playing with their autographed baseballs.

I'm sure Gabby's relatives would have been none too happy if they'd known such valuable memorabilia was being used this way. But for a couple of weeks in the summer of 1966, a bunch of twelve-year-old boys playing on an old sandlot meadow in a small town got to extend their season a little longer. Gabby would have been happy about that, too, I think.

For us major league wannabes, The Meadow was our Fenway Park, Yankee Stadium, and Wrigley Field all rolled up in one field of dreams. Hey, the Cubbies finally won the World Series this year! When we played baseball, we imitated our favorite players and made believe we were real big leaguers. We adopted batting styles and eccentricities of our favorite players. We chewed big wads of Bazooka Joe bubble gum and spit on the ground just like our idols. Many of these same idols were also smoking and selling cigarettes on television. I think we may have experimented with cigarettes because of these role models. But hey, that's the way things were back then.

The Meadow was our summer sanctuary where we felt safe and free to have as much fun as we wanted. It was our place—no adults allowed. The Meadow held the spirits of players, umpires calling out balls and strikes, and of complaining parents from previous generations who played there before us.

I've lived in California the past 25 years, but when I visit this little town every so often, I go by the old ball field and close my eyes and listen. I can still hear the birds chirping and the breeze in the trees. I recall the sounds of my buddies and me playing ball there. Those sounds are so clear I can easily visualize it as if it were just yesterday. The sound of a ball being struck by a wood bat is special, so unlike the ding sound made from a metal bat. I can hear the old-time infield chatter, not kids just standing in the field with expressionless faces hoping the ball does not get hit to them. And yes, a good old-fashioned umpire who yelled out balls and strikes without the demonstrative punch-out arm antics and spin-dance of umpires today. No wonder some players get upset at the umpire.

Sadly, the Meadow as we knew it as kids is not there anymore. It's just a big empty overgrown field. Maybe it was just meant to be. But I know there are people of all ages who go back there, to just sit, listen, and close their eyes to remember. So many names, faces, and memories are forever etched in my mind of the wonderful times I spent at the Meadow.

Getting the Ball Field Ready

In the spring, we would all get together and begin sprucing up the Meadow, getting it ready for a new season of baseball. It was an exciting time and a community project where everyone pitched in, as there was no budget for landscapers or funds to hire outside workers. The kids would pull weeds from the infield, dads would mow the outfield grass, and moms would bring cold drinks and snacks for everyone. Fresh dirt was brought in by a local landowner and was spread around the infield, pitcher's mound, and batter's box. Fresh chalk lines were laid out. The only thing missing was Good Ol' Charlie Brown warming up in the bullpen.

The outfield fences looked a lot farther away than they were but closer than the previous year. You could almost hear the voices of the old players and little leaguers from years gone by whispering in the clean New England air. You could imagine fans on the sidelines yelling things like "Sa-wing batta batta," "you're a bum," "c'mon Johnny, you can do it," and a few other choice words of criticism and encouragement from the peanut gallery.

This was our sanctuary. It was a sacred place where blood was spilled, sweat poured from our bodies on hot summer days, and badges of honor in the form of bruises from knocking down a line drive were earned.

Not everyone got a trophy back then—you had to earn awards back in those days. Our participation trophies were those bruises from stopping a hard one hopper with your chest or knee, or a hit by a pitch, one where you held back the tears as you ran to first base. They were badges of honor we wore proudly and with satisfaction showed off to the guys the next day. Nowadays, you hear some mom scream out, "Oh no, my poor little Johnny." Yeah, well little Johnny would not have lasted two innings with our bunch.

Hangouts

The Meadow was only one of our homes away from home. We had a few different hangouts we would go to after a ballgame or on a lazy summer day. One was the World War II Memorial Park in the center of town. It was on Main Street, close to the stores and a few of the other of our hangout areas. The park was dedicated to those who had served and died during the foreign wars. There was a big façade with the names of those from town who had given their lives in World War I and II as well as in Korea. The park was a large area with a big oak tree right in the middle. The tree must have been at least two hundred years old.

There were two large silver- painted cannons with plugged turrets and only steel rims for tires that dated from World War II stationed under the tree like bookends guarding the park. It was as if the old oak was a symbol of lasting life and the sentinel cannons reminders of man's capacity to destroy it.

The cannons got a fresh coat of silver paint once a year right before the Fourth of July parade. The paint also covered all the writings we inscribed on them. This was not graffiti like you might see today, as back then we did not paint vulgar graffiti, lewd pictures, or gang signs. Our little gang of pals did not have colors, hand signs, or any of the weird markings that stain cities and towns today. We usually penned our initials and those of whoever our girlfriend was that summer. "Tommy loves Betty" inside of a heart with arrow going through it was as about as bad as the artwork got. It was a good thing they painted over the cannons each year because, sure enough, we all had a new girlfriend by the following summer. Not like a tattoo today where you could be stuck with Betty for life.

We played tackle football at the park, with the oak tree and cannons on the sidelines near mid-field. They came into play at times and were often used as part of the offense or defensive strategy. The football playing area was long and narrow and it had more than a few hazards. There were dips in the terrain, a cement sidewalk on one side, and those blasted cannons on the other side. Many a reception or end run ended up with a little bit of cannon barrel in your face or a cement scrape on your knees.

At one end, there was a fence that bordered a nice big white house. If a pass to the end zone were badly overthrown, our football would end up in the front yard of the house where two scary looking dogs patrolled the yard just waiting to get their teeth into our football. The kid who threw the errant pass was the one who had to go in and retrieve the football. We always came armed with a few raw hot dogs, however, to lure the dogs away from the ball so we could resume our game.

It was nowhere near a regulation football field, but it served our purpose. In addition to the cannons, tree, and end zone hazard, the field sloped in one direction. Whoever had the ball that half going in the direction of the downhill slope had a big advantage. You had an even greater advantage if you had one of the big fat guys on your team. He would be a blocker when we were going uphill, but on the downhill slope he was like a freight train to bring down when he ran the ball. I was the skinny kid with the strong arm who could throw the football deep to the big guys, but I stayed away from the big guy running full speed with the ball downhill.

So, with a mixture of big guys, little guys, fat guys, and skinny guys, the games took on epic proportions and lasted most of a Sunday afternoon during football season. Come rain, snow, or shine we played tackle football. There were always enough guys wanting to play and the games went on all day, the winners holding the field. Sometimes guys from other towns would come to play. Town honor was at stake on those occasions and only the best players got to play those games.

We would wear our worst clothes when we played—torn pants, ripped shirts, and soiled sneakers were our uniforms. You could tell the better players by how tattered their clothes were, their shirts and pants were more ripped and their sneakers more soiled. This was full hands-on, no helmets, no holds barred— although there was a lot of holding—tackle football. There were no shoulder pads or mouth guards and we did not call time out for bloody noses. We would get bruised, scraped, and injured. This was the Millville version of rugby. Testosterone was in full throttle at this age of male adolescence—tempers would flare and scuffles ensued on occasion, and little guys would get flattened by larger ones without remorse.

But those same little guys were also harder to catch. Sometimes a big guy would hand off the ball to a little guy, push him in the middle of a group of bigger guys and it became a big blob moving forward. Many a touchdown was scored using this method, but it was usually the little guy's last play of the game.

We never had a real serious injury and no one ever went to the hospital, except for the one time when Fat David smacked his head on one of the cannon turrets. He got a nasty cut and I think it took ten stitches to close it. But Fat David walked around proudly for weeks showing off those stitches. It also made him look a little mean and nasty, so he was able to scare some of the out of town players.

Just like in baseball, the cuts and scrapes we got were our badges of honor and we wore them proudly. Who is going to mess with a kid who has bruises from playing sports? Today, too much is over-organized and parents do not let their kids out on their own playing contact sports without supervision and the latest in sports technology safety equipment.

Have you seen the little guys in all their pads and protection trying to move around? They can't even run or get up by themselves when knocked down. I think it is more dangerous today with the so-called organized sports. These kids have the latest equipment including super hard helmets, huge pads, and shoes with hard rubber spikes that can inflict a lot more damage than we ever could in our tattered clothes and soft-soled soiled sneakers.

There is too much coddling and "oh no, poor baby" syndrome going around, denying kids from having a little clean hard fun. I think every young boy should know there are going to be a few hard knocks in life. I am glad I learned how to get up off the ground, dust myself off, and get back in the game. Kind of like in real-life, huh? Maybe I'm just an old throwback from another time, but these early life experiences taught me well and prepared me for the future.

Chapter 3

Summer Fun

Leave Me Alone—I Just Wanna be a Kid

Summer vacation was a time for just being a silly kid. We needed to unwind from a tough school year and the long New England winter. We did not have video games, smartphones, or 500 channels on TV to keep us sofa-bound and atrophy our muscles. We didn't have our thumbs glued to cell phones all day with our heads bent down straining our eyes on a tiny screen. We socialized in person, moved around a lot, and you know, used our muscles.

We used our imagination to invent all kinds of things to do outside and found cool places where to go on adventures. Imagination was our iPod. We had real friends you could see, touch, and talk to. We didn't *unfriend* anyone unless we did it in person and had a good reason. A true friend was a gift, not a picture on a website or phone.

We did not tweet or text hundreds of times each day; we talked to each other in person. Our brain was our smart device (although mine did freeze up often enough and would have to be rebooted). We downloaded ideas from our imagination and played them out in our real time doing real things.

There was this one place, about a half mile into the woods right behind my house, where there was a hill with a lot of big rocks covered with moss. We had just seen *Robin Hood* at the movies and it was there that we re-enacted the epic of the heroic Robin and his merry men fighting off the evil Sheriff of Nottingham. Sometimes we even had a Maid Marian to save. But, most of time it was just us guys battling each other with wooden swords and throwing sod bombs at each other.

A confession: the wooden swords came from Miss Carson's white picket fence. We *would* always bring them back—unless we broke them; but there were always a few missing white pickets in her fence. We did always have enough sod bombs to fling around at each other, though. (Nowadays, if a kid merely points at another person, the lawyers are summoned.)

Summer Dances and Girls

My pals and I were all around twelve or thirteen years old when we first started to notice girls. Up until then, we did not think of them as anything other than the extra ball player or someone to goof on. I don't remember just when it happened, but we noticed the tight skirts and the tops of their shirts starting to stick out. They started wearing blue eye shadow, lipstick, and miniskirts. They were younger versions of the girls we saw in our first nudie magazines, but with clothes on.

Nevertheless, our imaginations ran wild and now girls were a big deal. A guy who would normally be a .450 hitter would strike out on three pitches once a few of these little cuties started hanging around the ball field smiling at him during the game. They should have been banned from all ballgames.

As for the guys, we were all rather dorky looking, awkward, and afraid to even talk to the same girl who just a year earlier we had made fun of. Now we could barely get two words out. There were a few cool guys, always combing their hair and real comfortable around the girls, but I wasn't one of them and neither were most of my friends. None of these girls were fainting at the sight of us. Again, how did The Beatles do that?

So now the tables were turned and we were the ones trying to attract a girl, hoping that one of them might talk to us. A guy without a girlfriend at this age was a problem. Everyone would think, "Who is this guy that no girl will hang out with or dance with him, never mind even consider kissing?" Unfortunately, there were quite a few of those poor fellows and they suffered through a difficult time in their life. Rejection is a terrible thing, especially when you're only thirteen.

But for those of us fortunate enough to sum up the nerve, we have a few fond memories of young love. I remember the Friday night dances at the house of one girl in town. Helen Clark lived in a large house and her parents were very nice. The house had a big room in the basement and they turned it into a place where we could get together on weekends. We would play records, hang out, and dance. They even served us food and soft drinks. There were plenty of chairs and sometimes a girl would come and sit with one of us. Sometimes we even got to kiss the girl. Mr. Clark looked the other way most of the time, but sometimes we would get a tap on the shoulder and hear Mr. Clark's deep voice say, "Okay, you two, break it up." But as soon as he would leave the room, the romantics would start up again. This was called "making out" in my day and "necking" in the 50s. I don't know what it's called today and really don't want to know. Maybe they kiss each other's face on the phone, I don't know.

When it came to dancing, the girls were much better dancers than the guys for the most part. A young girl doing the Twist looked a lot better than some skinny boy doing it. Our slow dancing left a lot to be desired and when we danced fast we looked ridiculous. We thought we were cool—swinging hips, spinning around, and feeling the beat, but we probably all looked very stupid. When we slow danced, it was pretty much just walking around very slow, trying to hold the girl as close as humanly possible without Mr. Clark's intervention. It would take a few more years to develop the cooler teenager moves.

CHAPTER 4

The Community

Who's Got the News?

Unlike today, up-to-the minute news and the latest information were not available unless you were glued to your three-channel television or transistor radio all day. What are transistors anyway? High-tech jargon of the day, I guess. Lacking today's high-tech gadgets, we had to wait until we got home to find out if anything important happened that day. Everybody usually watched the 6 o'clock evening news on the television during dinner. The newscasters, if you could see them through the cloud of cigarette smoke, were boring to us kids. They talked in low gruff voices, often coughing from the packs of cigarettes they smoked each day. They looked like your dad wearing cheap suit with a five o'clock shadow on his face. They were always way too serious, never smiled, and lost our attention quickly.

Like I said, we didn't know something had happened until hours or even days after it occurred. Walter Cronkite, Chet

Huntley, and David Brinkley were the only national newscasters we recognized. There were others, but these three were the top guys of our time, the kings of the newscasters. We depended on these guys for everything. It was Mr. Cronkite who told us JFK had been killed. Even as a young boy of nine, I remember the voice of Mr. Cronkite delivering that message on TV. He was very emotional and you knew something terrible had just happened.

Today, everyone knows the very minute anything important happens. It seems like every kid over the age of five has a smartphone or an iPad. You watch their little thumbs and fingers speeding across tiny keyboards text messaging, tweeting, Instagramming, emailing, or playing games. There are even times when they are communicating this way with someone standing right next to them. They walk around with heads down looking at their phones, bumping into things and other people while looking for the Pokémon. It doesn't matter where you are, the airport, a mall, or in school, you need to be careful looking out for someone using their phone to make sure they don't walk right into you or your car.

It's amazing. Whatever happened to kids playing card and board games? We did not sit in front of television all day, play video games for hours on end, or have our fingers and thumbs glued to high-tech gadgets. We had to rely on good old-fashioned resources for our fun, news, and entertainment.

We did have our own local news outlet with an entire team of not-so-humble correspondents, however. These self-assigned reporters were wired and ready for sound at a moment's notice. Gossip, innuendo, and hearsay were their version of Internet chat rooms and social networking in our little town. We called this organization the "Old Ladies Broadcasting Network" or station OLBN. Many an old lady in town took turns as editor in chief or keynote speaker, but they were always on assignment.

If they'd had Twitter back then, these old gals would have made millions of tweets and had thousands of followers.

We could be playing in our friend's backyard or just hanging out at the local convenience store and we could hear an OLBN reporter chatting about this person or that event. They were always ready for the next news flash or breaking story. They would talk about a flirtatious new single woman in town or the often-tipsy Mr. Potter. If anyone in town was thinking about buying a new car, within a few hours they would know the make, model, and how much it cost. And they would tell *everybody*. There was always a wide range of talking points, special reports, and news bulletins coming out of station OLBN. No one was safe and you had to be extra careful when they were around. I know my friends and I made the evening news quite often.

Small Town Comfort and Stability

As in most small towns, almost everyone knew each other and it was hard to keep anything secret for long. With station OLBN at the peak of its broadcasting power, local news traveled fast. No one in our little town ever signed an NDA and I don't remember anyone suing anyone else over trivial matters for money or spite. Sure, we had our gossips, busy bodies, and the unofficial court reporters, but there was also a sense of community spirit and togetherness. Many of the people I know today were born and raised in little towns just like ours.

People did not move as much as they do now and many settled close to where they had been born. Settling down with family and a job within a fifty-mile radius of where one was born was commonplace. I guess we had more of a sense of belonging and of being part of a community. Impersonal social events have replaced what was once closely knit gatherings held on special and not so special occasions.

We looked forward to our small town get-togethers and town hall dances where folks talked to each other, sharing stories and political wisdom. Moms prided themselves on their baking skills by making some of the best pies and pastries I've ever tasted. We listened to the old folk's stories and respected them. We loved to hear their "when I was a kid" stories. They were cool stories about growing up with very little but still having fun and getting by. What's a kid today going to tell his grandchildren? "When I was a young boy, I only had a 2 gigabyte iPad." Or maybe this one, "We went on vacation one time and the place didn't even have WiFi." That must have sucked, huh? Poor kids.

Our three-channel television didn't look so bad after learning what the older folks did for entertainment. Some of these oldsters were war heroes, successful businessmen, or just plain good folk minding their own business and helping when they could. We cherished these people and treated them with the respect they deserved.

There were other people in town that may have been strange and maybe even considered oddballs because of the way they talked or dressed. But they were still part of our small community and deserved to be treated with kindness and respect. Whenever any of these people would pass away, it seemed like a small part of the town disappeared, too.

I felt safe in this place called home for fourteen years of my life. I don't recall much in the way of crime—other than our little schemes here and there. No one's house that I knew of ever got broken into and no one's car was ever stolen. Heck, my father used to leave his keys in his car while parked in the driveway all night. I think that was because he was always losing his keys. He had a 1960 Chevy that didn't need a key to start it anyway. Yep, the ignition could be turned without the key in it; just turn the switch where the key went and the engine would start and off you went.

Funny thing though, he did manage to lock himself out of the car a few times with the key still in the ignition. You locked the doors of these old cars by pushing down the button on the inside top of the door and holding the push button in on the outside door handle while you closed the car door. There were those few mornings when I heard my father utter a few choice words, storm back into the house and ask me to help him look for something to break into his car. He usually used an old coat hanger to make a j-hook at the end of it. He would then snake the stiff hanger wire down inside the window and unlatch the lock from inside the door panel. I wonder where he learned that trick. Came in handy.

I think one of the reasons we had a peaceful easy feeling of security, and our home being safe and protected was because everyone had a dog. These were real dogs, not five-pound foo-foos that people carry around in their purse or shivering little fur balls my cat could beat up. These were not pedigree dogs, but were mostly those saved from the pound and thankful they had a home, one they would guard with their life if need be. Our dogs were big and would scare the daylights out of anyone coming into the yard after hours. We never tied up our dogs, so the fear of being chased down and eaten by one of these creatures had to be considered.

During the day, our four-legged friends traveled right alongside us, running with our banana seat bikes. They got into mischief along with us on our merry way. So, here we were, a half dozen ten to twelve-year-old boys on fast bikes with a pack of mangy mutts for protection. Not exactly easy prey for any would be evil-doers. Yeah, we were safe enough.

Memorial Day Weekend Parade

CHAPTER 5

Special Events

Parades and Stuff

I don't think many of the kids today experience special events and the holidays like we once did. Heck today, one group or another seems to be always complaining something offends them and our leaders cower to their nonsense. Need those votes you know. Not when I was a kid. Christmas was Christmas, just as were most all other holidays and observances dating back to the Founding Fathers.

I have fond memories of the annual events like the Memorial Day weekend parade, with all the town's groups and organizations marching proudly down Main Street. It was a simple but nice parade with people lining the sidewalks to watch. On this special day, scores of Little Leaguers, Girl Scouts, and Boy Scouts paraded up Main Street dressed in their clean and neatly pressed uniforms. We marched alongside the Veterans of Foreign Wars, local politicians in vintage cars, and the local high school marching band at the front of the parade.

Many of the older war veteran's uniforms did not fit very well any longer, but they were proud to march. (Hey, you think you still fit into your old high school tux or prom gown?) They saluted the flag and put their caps over their hearts when the National Anthem was played. No one kneeled in protest or disgraced the flag as some do today in the guise of First Amendment rights. Looking back, I can't help but thinking how lucky we were to have these old soldiers around to remind us what exactly that flag represents.

The town hall was a big building in the center of town. It was used for many public meetings and events, but what I remember most were the Saturday night dances during the summer. The second floor had a large open room where the dances were held and a stage at one end with an old piano where recitals and school plays were staged.

We would put folding chairs all around the perimeter of the dance area for guys and gals to sit. Most of the time, all the girls sat on one side of the room with the guys on the other. One brave guy would get up the nerve to walk over to the girls and ask one to dance. The absolute worst was getting "the shut-down," or in other words, being told no thank you by the girl you asked to dance. All too often, however, the girl did not say "thank you," it was more like "get lost" or "are you kidding?" That meant the guy had to walk back over to the guy section empty handed and be ridiculed by the less daring boys. Really, most of the girls were just as shy and secretly hoping someone, anyone, would ask them to dance a slow dance.

The guy with the best record player would bring it to the dance and spin everyone's favorite records. We would ask the DJ to play the fast songs most of the time just so we could watch the girls wiggle around in their mini-skirts.

We also held scout meetings at the town hall and even used

it for basketball. It served as the town's one-room police headquarters and even had a small holding cell for the notorious criminals the brave constables arrested. In addition, it was used to store the beer that was confiscated from the local teens, later to be divided up between the "administrators." Over the years, we bought those guys a lot of beer. The town's politicians and administrators also had small offices in the town hall where they conducted high level shenanigans—I mean business.

At the very top of the building there was a siren that sounded whenever there was a fire or some other emergency. A certain number of blasts from a very loud siren meant different things. Two short sirens meant there was a grass fire someplace, but seven long sirens meant someone's house may be burning down. One long loud blast was a call for someone to bring donuts to the firehouse.

Each summer the Little League held tag day. This was a time when Little Leaguers rode their bikes through town in search of donations to help pay for uniforms and equipment for the upcoming season. There was never any money or a budget for our sports activities, so we had to raise our own funds. We needed new uniforms every other year as well as baseballs, bats, catcher's mitts, and money to pay for umpires. Those umpires who were not paid usually ended up being some kid's dad who did not have the heart to call his own son out on strikes, and that would start the name-calling and eventually lead to the dad walking off the field, leaving us without an umpire. Never let dads umpire. The moms had a wider strike zone anyway and relished the power of the umpire.

So, like little tax collectors, we went door-to-door asking for money. In return for a small donation, we would hand out a paper tag stamped with the name of our team wrapped around a red paper rose with a green stem. The person was supposed to attach the tag to their clothing so the other little tax collectors would know they had already donated and not to hit them up again. That never bothered me—I often asked the same person several times during the day and would often see someone with two or three tags in their buttonholes.

We were polite and respectful, but did manage to put on our saddest face when asking for a donation. One of my favorite tricks was to take most of the donations out of the can each time I rang a doorbell. I would shake the can so that only a few coins would rattle to make it look like I had barely collected any money. I would show them the can with about eight cents in it and ask for a donation. Who could resist this little guy having a hard time collecting donation? Sometimes a person would feel so bad for me they would invite me in the house for milk and cookies. Worked like a charm every time.

The team that got the most donations got a small prize, but most importantly, bragging rights to having raised the most money. And for the first part of the baseball season anyway, we played with brand new baseballs and wooden bats that were not cracked and held together with glue and nails.

Tag day was supposed to be only one day each year. But we used to wait a few weeks afterwards and use the leftover tags we did not turn in and go collecting for ourselves. Capitalism at work.

Respect and Pride

The topic of respect and pride deserves more attention because I think there is a lot of room for improvement today. We certainly were not little angels, but we did respect our elders, most property, and we were proud of our country. I'm certain we knew more about our country than most kids do today.

We knew the name of every state capital as well as major rivers and dams across the United States. Okay, this may not get you into Harvard, but one should know a little about this country's history and major landmarks. Ask a kid today what the capital of Montana is and they may ask you "what is a Montana, is it related to Hannah"? And if you ask them about New England, they might ask if that is next to Old England.

Most times we knew right from wrong. We were not mean to old people and we did not destroy property. We saluted the flag at scout meetings and held our hand over our heart as we recited the Pledge of Allegiance each morning in school. A Christmas tree was not a holiday tree. The holidays we celebrated were traditional and true to our heritage and we respected each other's faiths.

Our holidays and beliefs were not held hostage subject to change because it offended certain groups with no knowledge to the founding of this country. I believe we grew up doing what our forefathers planned. I don't remember one person being offended or complaining about holidays, flags, or the word God printed on our money and etched on many public buildings. I guess that is what upsets my generation. We don't mind at all if someone with another belief does not want to participate in our traditions—but don't tell us we cannot celebrate them because they offend you.

Our parents were hard workers. Most of them worked for the same company for many years. They did all kinds of jobs and most of the companies they worked for were within a relatively short distance from home. There was no such thing as a bailout back then. If their company went bankrupt or failed due to lack of good products, mismanagement, or obsolescence, well that was just too bad, the workers would have to acquire new skills and get another job. The knitting mills, glass factories, and other businesses that became obsolete were not bailed out by the taxpayers. They went under, never to be seen again.

Our parents expected us to study hard and work to the best of our best abilities so that we could have a better life than theirs. Most of our parents grew up during the Great Depression in the 1930s, so they were tough and resilient. You think the 2008 Depression was tough?

Parents wanted their children to try and do the right thing whenever they could. Even though our dads were tough, hard guys, they expected us to defend the weak, protect the ladies, and to not back down from a bully.

The bully always got his payback back in the day. If a bully got the best of me or one of my buddies one day, he paid for it eventually by meeting up with two or three of my friends to remind him that being a bully was not going to work in our neighborhood.

Chivalry and a good Samaritan is hard to find these days. The fear of lawsuits for helping someone in need has made people hesitant to even lend a helping hand. Back then, whenever economic times got bad, our little community came together to help each other. If someone's dad got laid off from work, lost his job, or was injured, neighbors came together. Friends and neighbors would bring dinners or vegetables from their gardens to help a family in need.

People baked more back then and there were always great tasting homemade pies and muffins made from natural ingredients being offered. If someone had a certain pie or cake that was their specialty, it often came to be known as a certain mom or grandma's creation, like Mrs. Jones' blueberry cobbler, the best in town!

Nobody ever wanted a hand out or went looking for one. If you were capable, whatever the job, you took that path rather than being supported by the government. There were always a few of those freeloaders and lazy ones, but nothing like today. Today government is a major reason many people don't work and earn a wage. They can make more on the government dole and still have their wide screen television and cell phone!

Back in the day, it was a stigma to be on welfare or take food coupons. Although it is an important and needed service, it was a last resort for proud, capable families. Healthy, eager workers with job opportunities should not have to be paid for doing nothing. They should also not have their irresponsible debts forgiven and paid by hard-working men and women paying taxes.

Today, more people are on the government entitlements than ever before. Entitlements—what a ridiculous name to call these programs. Some need it and deserve it, but over fifty million people in the U.S. receive some form of public assistance as of this writing? This is not a safety net; it's a loophole that promotes fraud to devalue our country's generosity and good intentions.

My wife and I have been married for forty years. Thankfully, she never had to draw on unemployment benefits. I did once, right after we got married in 1976. That lasted about two weeks, as I took whatever job I could to get off that awful list.

It was an embarrassment back then to not have or take a job if one could. Today, people can lie around and collect money for being lazy and work under the table making tax free money. This is not the America I grew up in and I can only hope we can straighten it out before it's too late. Fifty million people—seriously? It will get worse before it gets better if not addressed.

Remember private donations and volunteer work? Private charities like The Jimmy Fund, Danny Thomas and St. Jude Hospital, Shriners, and the March of Dimes were trusted organizations. These and many other private organizations provided millions of dollars to help those in need. Now, donations are down because of corruption and people are no longer able to trust where their donations are going. Excessive administrative costs take up too much of the donation dollar these days, and in certain organizations only a small percentage goes to those who need it. There will always be people in need and thank God we are still a compassionate country with a big heart willing to give. I just hope we don't lose the capability to give.

In our little town, just about everybody's dad had a job and kids earned their spending money doing chores and odd jobs around the neighborhood. Most of us did not get an allowance. We were allowed to work if we wanted extra money to buy the candy, sodas, and comic books our folks would not let us waste *their* money on. Nowadays, these things are all part of the weekly shopping basket resulting in adolescent obesity and the rise in type 2 diabetes.

We were also expected to save some of our money, although that was always a challenge. If we wanted something bad enough, we saved for it. We tried to be creative, thinking up ways to sell something or provide a service someone might pay us for. And when we did this, no one bothered us because it was just some kids trying to make a little money.

Every now and then these days I see some kids in the neighborhood with a lemonade stand or kids next to the golf course selling wayward golf balls back to the same guy who had probably lost them during an earlier golf outing. These little businessmen and women make me smile, taking me back to a day when it wasn't against the law for a kid to sell a glass of lemonade. Nowadays, after a few days or even a few hours, some local official shuts them down because the poor kids don't have a vendor's license. I guess we need all the tax and fee revenues we can get these days.

Chapter 6

Back in the Day

Lagging Technology

I'll admit, small towns like Millville were somewhat sheltered back then and it took time for new technology to reach us. Heck, the morning newspaper did not arrive at the candy store until 2 or 3 PM most days. I know because I had to deliver about fifty newspapers every day on my paper route. Rain or shine I made sure people got their newspaper. I had two metal baskets fitted to the rear fender of my bike to carry the newspapers. I guess the extra weight helped build leg muscles that helped me run fast and jump high. Paperboys and girls were in great shape back then. Today they are extinct.

The people on my paper route had to wait for me to deliver the papers or go to the store and get their own paper. So, with me getting out of school at 3 PM, it meant most of the people did not start reading it until after suppertime! By that time, the news was almost two days old. If station OLBN had had a sports reporter or an old weather lady, no one would even have needed these so-called newspapers. They would have saved 10¢ each day and received up to the minute reports. (I just noticed, there is no cents sign on my keyboard. I had to search for it in the Word software and found it hidden amongst hundreds of other symbols. Is the penny not that important anymore? I read the other day where its cost our government 1.8 cents to even make a penny and a nickel cost 9.2 cents. How do they stay in business? Try getting a loan with that kind of business plan.

Like I said, modern day advances and new technology gadgets reached us later than in the bigger cities. Aside from the local TV repairman, who carried only a bag of odd-shaped tubes and a few strange looking parts, we did not have highly trained technicians around to install anything too complicated. Our dads often took things apart but rarely could put them back together in good working order. We usually couldn't afford the new devices anyway. Heck, only the rich people in town had those fancy remote control TV channel changers so they could surf through the three stations from the ease of their chair.

Talk about a simpler time? The trucks at the fire station were vintage 1940s and most everyone still had a party line telephone. Some of you may remember a telephone party line? What is that you ask? No, it's not when you want to throw a party and call everybody you want to invite. Okay kiddies, imagine picking up your cell phone and someone else is already on the line talking to another person. You would have to wait until they finish talking so that you could use your cell phone. I don't think you would do too well with that. Well, I guess you could always text them. However, the text button on our wall phone did not work back then. There was a hash tag symbol however.

The technological marvel of our day was the television set with its three wonderful channels. If you were one of the lucky ones, you had a color TV. Most of us had to get up off our butts from the sofa to change the channel using this big round knob on a front panel up in the right-hand corner of the TV. The big knob went clunk, clunk every time you turned it. Oh, I forgot, there was another clunk for the third channel. I think that's one of the reasons why we were thinner than today's kids—we had to move around more to do things! Even watching TV burned a few calories in my day. We must have jumped on and off the couch hundreds of times each day. That was a lot of moving around.

It surely was a time of innocence, one that most children today will never get to experience. We played imaginary games with homemade toys and ran around in the woods. We even played war in the woods running around with toy guns making believe to shoot each other. If you got caught by surprise, you were expected to take the bullet in your gut, do your best fake of writhing in pain and play out a convincing death or injury. Some of us could have won an Oscar for the scenes we played out. We even used to fill balloons with red food coloring and break them to make believe blood was spurting out all over. Imagine kids playing like this today. The lawyers would have a field day and the psychologists would have plenty of clients.

We used to make believe we were our TV heroes. Our TV idols came mostly from the Western shows and sports. But there were a few tough cops, like Chief Dan Matthews (played by Broderick Crawford) in *Highway Patrol* and a tough deep-sea diver named Mike Nelson (played by Lloyd Bridges) in *Sea Hunt*. For us guys though, our real heroes were the cowboys. We wanted to be just like those tough cowboys shooting their guns, riding fast horses, killing the bad guys—and always getting the girl at the end. We pretended to ride sidesaddle, shooting our rifles from underneath our horse at full gallop! So, big deal if we were just sitting on a fence. These white picket steeds were as real to us as are the life-like video game battles of today.

No one ever wanted to be the Indian, though. The Indians always lost and got killed, just like it really happened, I guess. We were never taught much of their plight and how unfairly the Indians were treated. No one talked about how the white man stole their land and took advantage of them. This was how mainstream America wanted their young people to see the world back then. We were sheltered from some of the harshest truths of our time. One good thing about today's information age is that the truth is harder to hide now. It's trying to figure out what the truth is and who to believe that is the hard part.

For the most part, I think most kids today are smarter than we were. I guess it's just a fact that as time goes by, better education and advances in technology breed higher intelligence over a broader spectrum. Today some kids are taking Algebra in middle school; we didn't start until high school. But I do believe we may have had a tad more imagination. We had to!

Kids today live in a high-tech world full of real-time information, fantastic learning tools, and even their toys are smart. But they also grow up much faster than we did. They have smartphones, sophisticated software that runs on advanced devices, and they have grown up with the Internet with the endless information highway at their fingertips. But, this easy access to information and interaction with so many people and things can be as harmful as it can be productive. The only thing our parents had to worry about was if we got our hands on a copy of *Playboy* magazine or were listening to the new rock and roll songs on our transistor radio too much.

Today, kids have iPhones, iPads, Blackberries, strawberries, and Halle Berries to keep them busy all by their lonesome selves. Who needs friends or a live person to talk with? And if you don't like your friend anymore, just click and they're gone. Everything is right there for them in a virtual world of endless and sometimes addictive activities. Internet video games, endless texting, tweeting, snapchatting, blogging, and chat rooms provide instant access to thousands of people. You don't need to move too far away from your double gulp soda and large bag of chips. I know I'm being cynical. But the sad thing is, this is an accurate assessment of how many kids spend their free time.

Kids today are zoning out from the high-tech gadgets and too much exposure to these devices is dangerous. Anyone can hide from behind a cell phone or computer screen and develop false senses of security. Remember the bullies I talked about earlier? Well, we could see them and punch them in the nose in my day. Now cyberbullies wreak havoc, causing emotional pain, and sometimes you don't even know who they are.

No one is safe today from anyone humiliating you for making a mistake. They have the ability to instantly challenge anything you say or claim by simply Googling it. Back in the day, I would say to my buddy, "Hey, Mickey Mantle hit 57 home runs last year." I thought I was right. I did not intend to mislead. He did hit a lot of home runs that year! Today someone can challenge my claim and in less than fifteen seconds call me a liar or just plain stupid. He can Google from his latest high-tech wireless gadget and correct me by saying, "I'm sorry Joe, but the Ole Mick hit only 52 home runs that year. If we are going to rely on you for accurate baseball data, please try to get your information right next time." For this minor error, my name and good reputation would be tarnished.

My mistake would be posted on Facebook, YouTube, and tweeted across the globe. It would follow me though my career, uncovered by human resource departments across the country. Who is this guy? I don't know about him. He falsified how many home runs Mickey Mantle hit. I embellish, but you get the point right? I swear, if one more person reaches for his phone to verify something I just said I'm going to punch him in the nose!

Lacking today's high-tech gadgets, we had to read actual books or go to the library to do research. Imagine having to walk into a big building with thousands of books in it? We even talked with the old folks and asked their opinion of historical events. We talked with people, read books, and wrote down information so that we could remember it.

It was funny how I always got stuck on the remembering part. I did well in things I liked and was interested in, but if I did not like a subject, I would stink at it no matter how many times I read the materials or wrote it out.

Our little library in town did not have computers and there was no WiFi. We were lucky to have a HiFi to play educational records. Ask a kid today what HiFi means. I guess he can Google it. Heck, I don't think there were even that many wires in the whole building. But I can tell you, Mrs. Durkin knew where every book, paper, record, or magazine was and when it was due back. I lost many a nickel paying back for overdue books thanks to Mrs. Durkin's uncanny organizational skills. She did not have a computer or an electronic way to manage the library. Her manual system of cards, reminders, and record keeping was perfection with no one ever disputing her late fees. Now I know why she kept bugging me every time she would see me, even years after I graduated high school.

While moving out of my parent's house when I was getting married, I found an old book from that library back in Massachusetts. This book was overdue by ten years. Luckily for me the library closed by this time and Mrs. Durkin retired. That would have been an ugly bill to pay.

Ch-ch-changes

A David Bowie song says, "time may change me, but I can't trace time." That is how I feel about the direction of our country. Our civil liberties are under attack, twisted, and reshaped for political gain, greed, and corruption. The future has lost the innocence of youth to those who wish to change our way of life forever, erasing a generation of hard workers and forthright thinkers.

The small-town feel and folksy pace of life we enjoyed is becoming a distant memory, taken over by increased regulations, government waste, and commitments to undeserving groups. Gone are the days when Norman Rockwell could step out of his car anywhere in this land and create a painting of a piece of Americana that was common to small towns and communities.

Our traditions are under attack. I cannot recall ever offending anybody by saying "Merry Christmas" or "God bless you." When we were punished by our parents and sent to our room, we had little to do there except maybe read a book or play a board game. Today, a kid almost wants to get sent to his room. Here, away from the scrutiny of parents, a kid descends into a technology-based fantasy world of physical inactivity, guzzling sodas, and munching on a mountain of saturated fats. Some punishment that is—play games and eat junk food.

I remember riding my bike all over the place without a care. We couldn't get into much trouble because everyone in town knew us. And we had to be extra careful around those we might have angered or upset in the past. Neighbors looking to get even with us would turn us in to our dad if we did something out of line. Some of the adults were worse tattle-tales than the kids. And don't forget the OLBN; they were always around.

During the summer my friends and I were together every day for most of the day. We would set out after breakfast, but only after doing a few chores around the house. We were expected back home for lunch around noon and then again for supper at 6 PM. Remember supper? That was a time when everyone sat at a table with real forks and knives to eat mom's home cooked meal. We did not eat food from greasy bags filled with hamburgers, French fries, or fried chicken.

Our mothers told us to "get out of the house, go outside and play, and don't get into any trouble." We were always glad to oblige them, but the last part was always hardest. On weekends we would go camping in the local woods and stay up most of the night having fun creating a little mayhem here and there. As long as we didn't get into any serious trouble and came home with minimal cuts and bruises, it was always okay. We cleaned ourselves up, thought up a few new pranks for the next excursion, and did it all over again the following weekend.

During the week, we would go through many daily summertime routines that I recall with a smile. They mostly consisted of hanging out, playing games, and just having a good time with friends and family.

I miss my old friends, the corny characters in the funny little town, and our favorite haunts. I miss the safety and comfort lost in the time capsule of our innocence. I want to be twelve again, transported back to those wonderful days when life was full of simple pleasures, surprises, and things one could depend on. I want to go back to a time when we were satisfied with less and happy to walk instead of ride.

This was when time and eternity intersected at the crossing lane of youth. And to think we got to act on this great stage every day, an adolescent venue of circumstance resulting in some of the greatest performances of our time. We were the stars of major production movies and did not even know it. Oh, what the generation of today is missing. They are missing the making of memories and life experiences!

Well, that sets the scene of how life was back when I was a young boy in a small town in New England. This is how it was, how people thought and carried themselves. My goal is to provide a little insight into the attitudes and ideologies we shared. We were not always politically correct and could have used a few lessons in proper etiquette. But I hope these little stories provide you with a few smiles, a few raised eyebrows, and rekindle some fond memories of a day gone by.

It took me 49 pages to set the stage, but times were so much different then. Now finally, my stories and adventures of Growing Up Small!

Ray's Service Team in Millville

CHAPTER 7

Stories and Adventures

The Ball Field—Big Guys and Little Guys

Living right across the street from the local ball field was a dream come true for a nine-year-old kid who had just moved in from the city. At first, it was touch and go as the kids made fun of me and made me feel like the outsider I was. I had a funny sounding last name and I went around with a big chip on my shoulder. I was mad about leaving the city and the few friends I had made there.

I was in the third grade when I arrived in this strange little town, and I faced many challenges as the new kid on the block. At first the kids were mean to me and made fun because I had lived in the nearby city that had a bad reputation. I had a hard time fitting in and was a loner for a while. But when it came time to play sports, I stood out. That is when I started to make my mark and with it a few good friends.

I was blessed with a strong throwing arm honed from throwing a few million pitches with a rubber ball against a stone wall in the city. I would pitch against imaginary batters, keeping track of balls and strikes thrown into a chalk-drawn square on the wall. I can't tell you how many times I struck out Willie Mays and Hank Aaron. I once fanned Mantle, Maris, and Mays six times in a row.

For me, baseball was a natural and the local kids finally took notice of my athletic skills. Shortly, I was being picked for teams and even the big guys wanted me on their team. I could run fast, throw a baseball hard, and was a good fielder. I could throw a football far, shoot a basketball with the best of them, and loved hockey on the local ponds. So, there it was, my opening, I had an in with the kids despite being the new guy in town. There was always room for a good player to help your team win.

Speaking about a good player, in 1966 I was in my last year in Little League. We had a good team, but only nine guys. It was a small town and having nine guys each night was not guaranteed. So, when someone was a no show, we had to play short and ended up with two kids playing the whole outfield.

My neighbor Jane was a good athlete and always played baseball with us in pick-up games. She was good too—for a girl. First mistake, just because she was a girl didn't mean she couldn't play. So, when we were short-handed, we would ask her to play on our Little League team. She did this for about six games. She was getting a lot of hits and playing a great first base—until one of the dad coaches started complaining. He said that girls had been banned from Little League back in the 1950s. The rules were checked and verified that a girl could not play.

Come to find out that back in 1950, a girl named Kathryn "Tubby" Johnston Massar cut off her braids, stuck her hair under her cap and became the first girl to play Little League baseball. That led to the rule barring girls from playing. There must have been some upset dad coach who did not like seeing his son bested by a girl. That rule was overturned in 1974, but too late for Jane who I know would have been one of the greats. She went on and did well in woman's sports, but she really could compete with the guys anytime.

Living across from the ball field was a huge advantage for me. All I had to do was look out the front window to see if any of the guys (or girls) were down there getting ready to play baseball. My ball, bat, and glove were always at the ready because teams were picked up fast and the games started quickly; hence, the origin of "pick-up" games.

The two best players we had were the captains and they chose sides by using a baseball bat. Starting at the barrel end of the bat, one would take turns with the other captain by putting fist over fist until whoever's fist landed last on the top of the handle got to pick first. The best players were chosen quickly and the lousy ones were left for end.

I never wanted to be left out because games went on for hours and if the teams were full already, I would have to wait for the next game. These were not your 9-inning baseball games. These games took on epic proportions. They could go on for 26 innings, 34 innings, or more and last from morning until the sun went down. There were hours and hours of battling back and forth until someone had to go home. Last bats never turned out to be last bats, and always resulted in an extra inning that turned into even more extra innings. It was never last bats. Complete darkness was last bats.

Sometime the baseballs got so beat up we had to quit because you could not even hit them anymore. We never had many good balls to start with, and only once in a while would get to use a brand new one. Sometimes the cover of the ball would start to unstitch and eventually come off. We would tape the ball with medical or electrical tape and continue to use it until it became too warped from the barrage of hitting. Also, you couldn't really throw a good curve with an electrical tape wrapped ball; it would come in to the plate like a big black bowling ball. At least it was something.

So just getting to the game and being at the right place at the right time was important if you wanted to play. I became good at hurtling chairs and jumping over couches and the dog on my way out the door to the ball field. Down the stairs I would run and across the street, dodging cars with reckless abandon. That's where I developed my speed, agility, and quickness. Well that, and from running away from my mother with her wooden switch. Don't know what a switch is? I'll get to that in another story.

The guys I grew up with ranged in age, physical makeup, and personality. None of them were close to being the sharpest tool in the shed. In fact, most could not even get inside the shed left outside to rust. Hey, it was a small town with little to do. You can only read so many comic books.

Anyway, there they were, etched in my mind like a painting, the *big guys* and the *little guys*. The big guys were, well, bigger and older than my friends and I. But still, they needed us little guys to round out ball teams and to make two or even three sides of nine players each to play a game of baseball.

There were no designated hitters back then. That did not come until 1973 with Ron Bloomberg of the Yankees. You can fact check me and Google it.

The big guys needed us, but not just for rounding out teams. They also needed minions upon whom to exert their superiority and sometimes brutality. They made us do a lot of stupid things and generally just took advantage of us. There were those times, though, when they needed us for other reasons. Sometimes one of us little guys had the newer baseball or better gloves and bats. So, in exchange for letting them use our stuff, we got to play on their team. Naturally we batted last, played right field, and had to bring the sodas.

But, playing with the older guys helped us hone our baseball skills and taught us valuable life lessons. Those of us who played baseball with the older boys ended up being a little better than others in our own age group. We excelled not only in developing higher skill levels in different sports by competing with older guys, but we also developed social skills that helped shape our character.

Often these big dummies, acting the way did, taught us what *not* to do, what not to say, and how not to act. Learning to deal with adversity and challenges toughened us up, providing us with street smarts most kids today just don't have.

Now, keep in mind, my friends and I were only ten to twelve years old and the big guys ranged from fifteen to nineteen years old. Some even drove cars to the ball field. That was way cool to us. Most of them smoked cigarettes and they introduced us to our first taste of beer and our first look at nudie magazines.

Sometimes they would get into fights with each other and we would all gather around in a circle to watch them battle it out. We would root for our favorite big guy and that, of course, led to our own smaller version of how to settle arguments, resulting in more cuts, bruises, and torn pants.

When we got home, mom would be mad but still treat our battle wounds with a kiss and a smile. Dad would peek up from his newspaper with that grizzled look of his, asking what happened and if I had won the fight. If I had lost the fight and been beaten to a pulp, he might be upset that somehow I had shamed him by not whipping the other boy.

I think I had a fifty-fifty batting average when it came to the scuffles I got into back then. But I always managed to avoid major injury and not get any long-lasting cuts or bruises. Some guys would end up with scars resulting in life-long nicknames to match the injury. I managed to be a straight up guy and maintain friendships even with guys I did not like that much. A good punch in the nose will do that, you know.

Like I said, if we did get in fights or trouble, mom cleaned our minor cuts and bruises, and then kissed us on the head. We would try to not make mention of these events when dad came home. In a small town, word got around fast if you got your butt kicked and that would not stand with most of the dads. Mr. Williams on Elm Street would always be the first to ridicule the kid who got beat up, "Hey Tommy, I hear Peterson cleaned your clock." Not all the grown-ups in town were real adults. I did notice that Mr. William's nose was permanently bent to one side. I wonder...

The big guys had many different personalities and tried to take on the persona of the tough guys in the movies. James Dean, for one, created a wave of wannabe tough hoods. Some of these guys had a cigarette pack of Lucky Strike rolled in the short sleeve of their white t-shirt tucked into tight blue skinny denim jeans. Others wore dark sunglasses and always seemed to have a long piece of grass sticking out between their two front teeth. Or they would sit atop the hood of a car with a cigarette hanging off to one side of their mouth and a beer in their hand. These were their props to look cool and act tough. But they weren't all tough.

There were actually a few wimpy big guys, but still, their mission in life was to pick on the small guys. They too were targets of the tougher big guys so they needed someone of their own to pick on. If you had an older tough brother or cousin, however, you were somewhat protected. The youngsters with no older siblings were fair game. This was our rite of passage.

A few of the big guys were somewhat nice to us, but most were mean-spirited, crude, and very stupid. Some were seventh- or eighth-grade dropouts. I'm talking doorknob stupid. Some of these dropouts looked ten years older than they really were. One guy I knew had gone to reform school and another had been kicked out of his house by his parents.

This one guy, we'll call him Wild Bill, was about sixteen years old and as big as a house. He'd been shaving since he was twelve and was 180 pounds of pure brawn and strength. He had a full beard and was buying beer at the local liquor store since he was fourteen. He turned out to be the neighborhood peacekeeper and broke up many a scuffle by tossing combatants by the seat of their pants to one side or another, ending minor squabbles quickly.

It wasn't long before we were all growing up and soon my little gang of buddies was the new big guys. A lot of the older guys left town—they went to Vietnam, prison, or just disappeared. It became our time for picking on the new crop of little guys, with us sitting on cars, smoking cigarettes, drinking beer, and looking at nudie magazines. Ah, the good old days.

Baseball and My Transistor Radio

Almost every kid my age had a transistor radio, but we usually just called it a *transistor*. It was like today with every kid having a cell phone. These radios ran on a single 9-volt battery. The batteries back then weren't so good and they didn't last very long, but then the radios weren't that good either. Most of them were made in Japan at a time when "Made in Japan" was not the greatest thing as far as quality went. Back then it meant the product was cheap, shoddily-made, and would break easily. Needless to say, you had to pick your spots to what you listened to or have a good supply of 9-volt batteries.

One of my favorite things to listen to was late night baseball. From the time I was seven years old I have been a New York Yankees fan. It was tough to pick up the New York station on my transistor way over in Massachusetts, but there was always a faint signal and I was able listen to some of the greatest teams in history.

The 1961 Yankees were one of the best teams ever assembled. They were sure to be in the World Series again and both Roger

Maris and Mickey Mantle were chasing Babe Ruth's single-season home run record. Roger hit 61 that year and broke The Babe's record. Mickey finished with 54 homers, finishing second to Roger in the MVP voting as well. A walking Google I am.

Earlier that year, my dad took me to my first major league baseball game. We made the long trip to Yankee Stadium in the Bronx, New York in an old yellow school bus, a trip that took over three hours. Once there, Yankee Stadium was like a dream world. It was magnificent—the House that Ruth Built! I ran down to the box seats next to the field where some of the players were signing autographs before the game. Mickey Mantle, Roger Maris, Yogi Berra, Whitey Ford! This was my first glimpse of professional ball players in person. I could almost touch them. I never did get an autograph, but their faces are etched in my memory. How could a seven-year-old kid in 1961 not like the Yankees! Fifty-six years later, well, I'm still a Yankees fan. My wife is a Red Sox fan so I guess opposites do attract.

So, from that day on, each night during baseball season, when I was supposed to be in bed for the night, I would wait until it was safe, turn on my transistor radio, which had been secretly stashed under my bed mattress, and listen to Yankees baseball. Mel Allen, Phil Rizzuto, and Red Barber were the announcers. I had to play the sound very low so as not to attract any attention. From under my bed covers and with one ear pressed to the tiny speaker of the radio, I listened to the games.

There was always a lot of static and the announcers' voices would fade in and out. In between the voices and static were also weird noises that ranged between a low hum and a high pitch. Sometimes the high pitch sound would hurt my ear and I would yell out in pain. The cause of these reception noises was the low-tech transistors inside the radio doing their best to capture the signal from over 200 miles away. I could hear the faint roar of the crowd and knew something important had just happened.

Pressing the radio closer to my ear, I would be able to hear the score or if Mickey had hit a home run.

These were my bedtime stories. Most nights I would fall asleep with the radio on only to wake up to a dead battery. When I did manage to stay awake and listen to the entire game, it showed the next morning. Mom would ask me if I slept all right and if I felt okay. Dad would just ask me "who won the game last night"? Some dads were like that back then. They knew you were goofing around, but it wasn't too serious so they had your back most of the time. Transistor radios and Yankees baseball—a joyous time for a young boy.

The Giant Goldfish

One summer, my friend, Eddie, and I were down by the Blackstone River messing around when we noticed reddish colored fish swimming in the water. They were red carp and there were lots of them, big ones and small ones. We went home and got our fishing poles, but we found that we could not catch them with worms or the fishing lures we had. We didn't know these fish were vegetarians. Well, we finally figured out that we could catch them with a piece of green felt on a hook, just like catching frogs for the annual freeway derby (a story for another time).

Anyway, we were able to catch these cool looking fish easily now. We did this for a while until the novelty wore off, which for a ten-year-old boy was about fifteen minutes. We brought a few fish home, thinking mom would be proud of us, but mom said they were not good to eat so we took them back to the river. We liked these fish, however, and wanted to be able to play with them, so we put them into pails of water and took them to our little brook near our house where we created our own little Sea World.

The little brook was perfect for our fish. The brook ran down from a big pond where we played ice hockey during the winter and it meandered for about a mile until coming to a place where we used to catch frogs, small brook trout, and snakes. Yes, we caught snakes. We dammed up one end of a section of the brook and created a little reservoir, a perfect holding area for the big gold fish. We made sure that water was always running through openings in the dam-like structure we constructed so there would be plenty of oxygen for them to live.

We put in about twenty fish and fed them lettuce and watercress from the brook. This went on for about three weeks and the fish started getting bigger and bigger. We kept feeding them and they kept eating whatever we gave them. We fed them lots of lettuce, carrots, and almost anything we had on hand. Those fish got huge! We had to increase the size of reservoir, expanding it to a large-scale water control project.

Soon station OLBN caught wind of what we were doing and we started to get daily visitors. We even charged little kids a nickel to see our fish. Eventually, we had to decide if we were going to keep the fish there or take them back to river. We finally decided to do the right thing and return them to their home in the Blackstone River.

The day we were planning on moving the fish, a guy stopped his car nearby our little brook project and walked toward us. He had a camera and I thought we were in big trouble. Maybe these fish were part of some secret government plan and we interfered. There were always secret government plans back then.

It turned out the man was from the local newspaper and he had heard about our natural gold fish bowl. He took our picture with the fish and ran a story in the paper about two kids who had discovered giant goldfish! It was very cool and we were famous for a few days. I know this story is on microfilm somewhere in that local paper's archives. I hope I can find it someday to show my kids and grandchildren of the time when my friend and I discovered Giant Goldfish!

Chapter 8

Moms and Dads

Dads Back in the Day

Let me tell you about dads back in the day. In the Sixties, especially in blue-collar families, guys were of a different breed. Nothing against dads today; many of today's parents are great, but for sure, they are, well, let's just call it, more politically correct. I hate the new PC environment we live in today, but hey, that's the way it is now. Respect, is one thing, but you need to respect my rights, views, and culture as well.

Many of my friend's dads fought in the Korean War and some even in World War II. Most of them had a scar on their face and many were missing fingers or other body parts, either from combat or some dangerous work-related injury in a nearby factory. The Occupational Safety & Health Act (OSHA) was not passed until 1970, so the men who worked in factories in those days did so at their own risk. They operated dangerous looking machinery with noise levels that made most of these men half deaf by the time they reached forty.

My dad worked at a knitting mill for forty years as the foreman and he was a pretty tough *hombre* in his time, never taking any crap from anybody and quick and able with his fists if he had to be. He was a brawny guy who could keep the crew in line to get a good day's work out of them. He was also the only one of the bunch who could add, multiply, and subtract. The best and the brightest did not work there at the mill.

Sometimes, not often, I would visit my dad at the mill. I'd bring him a sandwich and try to bond a little, but it was tough. One day he gave me and a few of my friends a tour of this 1940s-era knitting mill where he had worked most of his adult life. The Falls Yarn Knitting Mill on the Blackstone River was typical of factories of that era. Like many other factories during this time, polluting the river with various chemicals and harboring unsafe working conditions went unnoticed. The EPA was not formed until 1970 and many of the rivers and streams in and around cities were being polluted.

Once inside the factory, we saw an array of scary looking machines with pointy steel blades and spikes rolling and darting out in all directions. Loud booms and screeching noises made us jump at each turn. Big red buttons were everywhere. They were put there to try and stop any one of these monster machines from gobbling up a worker who made a wrong move. I believe the need to stop these contraptions occurred often, but only after it had hacked off more than one guy's finger or maimed a hand. This place looked like a chamber of horrors to me.

The red yarn being spun from the machines left a red stain color that looked like blood trails from mutilated body parts from past accidents. I was waiting for Vincent Price to step out from behind any one of these menacing devices, grab and throw me in to be cut to shreds. This was not a place for sissies. It was also not a place for any sane person to be working at, either.

The men who worked there had little choice in their livelihoods. They were mostly uneducated, with little or no prospects at safer or more gainful employment. No wonder my dad wanted a little peace and quiet when he got home. He was lucky enough to have survived the day. I think the main reason he wanted me to see this insane asylum was so that I would do well in school and get a better job than he had.

So, to say our neighborhood was a blue-collar segment of society was indeed an understatement. I think a better description would be a black and blue-collar community. Like I said, most of the dads did not attend college and most of them had barely graduated high school. They lacked social skills and were loud and ill-mannered most of the time. These were not men of thin skin. They had little patience with a short fuse that lit a quick temper. Like their fathers before them, they were there to put food on the table, a roof over our heads, hopefully pay a few bills, and keep the boys in line.

"Shock and awe" may have been a phrase coined by President Bush during Desert Storm and the War in Iraq, but that strategy was one used by the dads in my neighborhood long before Bush ever uttered the phrase. I swear, a squad of the dads from old my neighborhood would have beaten the crap out of Saddam Hussein and all his henchmen. And there would not have been any rules of engagement—just seek and destroy, like in the good old days. These days, we need to be careful we don't insult our enemies or hurt their feelings before we try to kill them.

As a kid growing up, we never wanted to mess up too badly before dad got home from work, either. Messing up on the weekend when he was right there to deal with you was bad enough. But messing up on a workday and having to wait until your dad got home could be really bad. We never knew what kind of day he had just had. He could have had a good day or a bad day, but most times it was a bad day. How many good days can one have working at the Mill from Hell trying to keep a bunch of derelicts in line?

Again, we never knew what kind of mood he would be in when he came home, so if we screwed up during the day, it was always mom saying, "Wait until your father gets home." That was some of the longest waiting and it usually did not end well for me. By the way, it was never "wait until your mother gets home." Moms were just the messengers of doom. But after it was all said and done, my dad was a fair man and handed out punishment to fit the crime. Some of my friends were not so fortunate. Still, the fear factor was enough to keep us on our toes.

Most of those neighborhood dads also received a level of respect throughout our small town. These were no-nonsense guys who didn't understand the cultural changes and attitudes happening in the Sixties. For a long time, twenty years or more, things had not changed very much in America. Men went to work, to war, they got married, and raised families. Politicians were always crooks and the rich always seemed to get richer. Technology was slow and the cars were always these big gas-guzzling beasts. Music started to change a little in the Fifties but nothing like what was coming.

These guys did not like hippies, the new music, or the fact that the Yankees were in last place that year. Their world was turning upside down and they were having a hard time with it. Vietnam was unfolding in front of their eyes and they became part of the prejudice that spurred ill-feelings between Americans, Southeast Asians, and American draft dodgers who headed to

Canada. I was twelve years old. My friends and I did not invent the derogatory names for Vietnamese and the draft dodgers; it was my dad's generation who lit the fires of prejudice. I guess they were upset and frustrated at the changes going on all around them. Hippies, LSD, and marijuana were just too much for this whiskey drinking, beer guzzling bunch of macho men from another era.

As kids, we were even afraid of each other's dad back then. Was it fear or was it respect? No, it was fear. We knew they had each other's permission to kick our butts if need be. Imagine that, Johnny's dad could give you a kick in the ass if you screwed up bad enough around him. And, your dad would be okay with it. He would probably have said "Thanks, Frank, for kicking Joey's ass for throwing the football through your window."

I do not remember things like that ever happening and I never did get a boot from some other dad, but it was always in the back of my mind. It certainly was a deterrent, so maybe these guys did have critical thinking skills. Maybe they all belonged to an organization or club, like perhaps the Secret Order of the Despot Dads. Anyway, the strategy worked most of the time.

Dads back in the day even looked dangerous. Many of today's dads are afraid of their wives. But these guys, no way. They looked a lot like the guys on the black and white FBI most wanted posters in the post office. And when they did put on a suit and tie, they looked just like the old gangster movie guys.

My dad and his buddies looked a lot like an unshaven Humphrey Bogart or a wisecracking James Cagney. They all looked alike with that hollow, sunken look in their eyes, just like Bogey in all those gangster movies. Often, they had five o'clock shadows and were tired-looking after coming home from work. They would walk into the house with a cigarette hanging out of the side of their mouth. Most of the dads back then smoked cigarettes, drank hard liquor and lots of beer, and were liberal with the English language.

They did not smile much, either, and only laughed when some other guy was having a hard time. Most of them just looked weird, staring into space a lot, with cigarette smoke coming out of their nose and mouth like the exhaust from some old car. They may have been dreaming about what it might have been like to have been able to go to college or maybe just being successful at something. I wondered if their thoughts were about if life had turned out just a little different and better for them. For most of these guys, it just didn't work out.

Many were shell shocked from the Great Depression in the 1930s and the wars overseas. And for those of us who were left to live with them, well, I guess we made the best of it. For me, I can't complain. Yes, I grew up a little on the dark side, but I married a great gal, raised a nice family, and am truly happy.

For most of the dads of the day, there were more down days than up ones. They were Depression Era men, many lacking any significant education, short in supply of life tools and inspiration to better themselves. They were just trying to survive and get through each day. I can't say they did the best they could, because no one will ever know if they ever tried that hard. Money spent on wine, whiskey, the racetrack, and woman should have been saved for more important things, like family and the future. Unfortunately, the future for most of these guys was not bright.

As soon as they came home from work, they opened a beer, lit a cigarette, grabbed the newspaper, and wanted to be left alone for a while. They may have kissed their wife on the way in and said hello to you, but it was a far cry from Ward Cleaver coming home from the club with his golf clubs on his shoulder in *Leave It to Beaver*. These guys figured they had earned a little time to be able to come home and relax for a few hours.

The last thing we wanted to do was get into any trouble that would tick them off. A bad report card, breaking something around the house, or causing another dad to complain about you was a prescription for disaster. But you know what? It was never as bad as we thought it was going to be. I know my dad did much worse things when he was my age. So, he would put on his bad guy face, growl at me, and send me to bed or something. But he would eventually come in later, sit on my bed and talk to me about how I should try to learn a lesson or watch out the next time. Those were some of the best times I had with my dad. Imagine, him trying to tell me how to watch out for myself. I only wished he'd taken his own advice.

But you know what, most little guys my age also thought their dad was invincible and the toughest guy in town. Even if he was just a working stiff and you did not see him much, your dad was the main man in your life. "My dad can beat up your dad" was always a topic of discussion when it came to family honor. We held these imaginary battles of our dads fighting each other, predicting winners and losers.

Now Tommy's dad, all five foot two and 135 pounds, he's a dead man. There is no way he was ever going to win any fight, even a made up one. Heck, he couldn't even beat up Tony Scala's grandmother. Scala's dad, on the other hand, was six foot two inches and about 270 pounds. Nobody took on this guy. Nobody except my dad, of course. My dad beats everybody. He never lost a fight and to me was the toughest guy in all of Massachusetts.

The mystery of the father and son relationship still confounds me. Pride, fear, respect, and disappointment all rolled up in one package of one's own imagination. I wonder if that is still the case today. I don't think so, because after all, doesn't everyone get a trophy these days?

Small Town Moms

My mother had a voice that could be heard throughout the entire neighborhood and Southeastern Massachusetts. She would open a window and bellow out my name so loud it sounded as if there was an air raid or the town was burning down. "Joeeey, Joeeey" she would yell at decibels not reached by an F-16 fighter jet or Harley Davidson motorcycle at full throttle. And across the street, about a quarter mile away, from my position at second base in the middle of a baseball game, I'd freeze in embarrassment as my buddies laughed and busted my chops as mom continued screeching my name, "Joeeey, Joeeey"!

Where were the cell phones? I needed an iPhone, an app... anything to quell that voice and the echoing sound of embarrassment. She could have text messaged me or Tweeted me—anything other than that voice echoing over miles of open space to the sacred ground where I sought sanctuary. Anything would have been better than the ridicule coming from my pals. This was the same woman who practically told me to leave town for the day on a Saturday, and here she was screaming at the top of her lungs just checking up on me or looking for me to come home when I was right across the street!

But, I guess she loved me and she wanted to know I was safe. I was safer than the President of the United States but never safe enough for mom. Come to think of it, President Reagan probably would have never gotten shot if my mom had been watching out for him. "Ronnie, Ronnie" she would have yelled at the top of her lungs. Hinckley never would have gotten close to old Ron if mom had been on the job. He would have eaten a whole lot better, too! Nancy was so skinny. She couldn't have been much of a cook.

Italian moms in the day had great power over the family and doled out punishment to unruly kids with the aid of a switch. Remember I mentioned a switch? My mother's version of a switch was a long, thin, and wispy branch from a willow tree in the back yard. When you think about a graceful willow tree swaying softly in the breeze, you imagine beautiful branches swaying back and forth to the tune of the wind.

Cut to the proper length with the leaves scaled back, however, these poetic appendages of nature were turned into formidable weapons and a deterrent to bad behavior. Darth Vader and his light saber would not have stood a chance against my mother twirling her switch. She could make vapor circles in the air and target a kid's behind so accurately it would have made Zorro look like a novice swordsman. Don't know Zorro either, huh? Google him.

I swear smoke would plume from that wispy branch as she twirled figure eights over her head. It was like the dance of death for my cousins and me. She would have made short work of both Vader and Zorro. When she was mad, fire came out of her eyes, her hair was flailing coal black, and she was yelling words in Sicilian that to this day I still do not know what they mean. Even the pets ran away in fear. All I knew was that it was going to be bad for me.

I'll tell you, get a dozen or so pissed-off little Italian ladies together with switches and they will clean out a gang of evildoers in no time. Skin Heads would be flying and tattoos bleeding from the onslaught of these portly maniacs in kerchiefs and wedge shoes. I believe a swat team of these crazed women, armed with their switches could clean up the south side of Chicago overnight.

My mom was a good cook. No, correction, my mom was a *great* cook! Aren't all four foot ten fat little Italian ladies? You bet your buns they are! All my aunts were small in stature but they were all good cooks as well.

Growing up with these great, unknown chefs and such fantastic food, I didn't know there was any difference and thought every kid ate as well as I did. Great pasta, meat sauces, homemade pizza, fresh fish, and chicken dishes were standard cuisine in my family. Just thinking about her steak pizzaiola, chicken parmesan, and spaghetti with real meatballs makes my mouth water! The fish dishes were very good, often made from flounder or rock bass we caught in the ocean over the weekend. I couldn't fathom food being served of any less quality or in any less abundance than mama's cooking.

That was until I ate supper one night at the O'Leary's house.

I'm not stereotyping here or referring to the content-less Irish cookbook here, but things were different in their household. The O'Learys were a nice Irish-American family and Mikey O'Leary was my best friend. Good kid, played third base, kind of skinny though. After eating at his house, I knew why he was so thin. Mrs. O'Leary kept a nice, neat home and the kids were always well dressed, but the food, my God, the food was terrible. It was the worst. How could these people survive on this?

I remember one day being invited over for supper. (There's that word again. And in New England it's called *suppa*. Okay, let's be PC and call it dinner.) I was outside playing catch with Mikey and his mother called us in for dinner. I sit down next to Mikey hoping for some good meatballs, linguini, a great tossed salad, and a nice piece of cake for dessert. Needless to say, that was not happening on this night. The food was tasteless and called boiled this or boiled that, I forget. And there wasn't any salad or a piece of cake afterwards. Who were these people?

Now I understand why my mom said that Mrs. O'Leary's oven was the cleanest in town.

Meanwhile, back at home I knew mom was cooking up a storm. It was a Friday night and a good meal was in store. Even though my two siblings had long before left the roost, mama cooked the same amount of food every night for just my dad and me. There was always enough food to feed at least six or seven people. So, each night around suppa time, a predictable cast of hungry characters would conveniently show up at our house.

They took advantage of my mother's big heart and friendly nature. It didn't matter who it was: the mailman, the milkman, the oil man making a late delivery, the paperboy on his last round, the guy next door fighting with his wife and not getting any dinner that night. These were my mother's steady customers. Cousins, uncles, friends, and even some foes eventually all gathered around mom's supper table to experience her gift of giving and great homemade Italian food.

Some of the other moms in the neighborhood were jealous of mom's great cooking. Sometimes their husbands would wander over around suppertime to borrow something (certainly not my dad's tools) and they would stay for supper, not just to be neighborly, but more out of not wanting to eat at home.

There is one guy, we'll call him Mr. Smith out of respect for his wife. He installed the very first home smoke alarm in our neighborhood. He said it was for safety in case there was a fire, but we all knew better. It was the Smith's family dinner bell. When that thing went off at the Smith's house, we all knew it was suppertime. Mrs. Smith's meals were always bad, but when the fire alarm sounded, Eddie and Timmy Smith knew they had to go home. The poor Smith Brothers. When that smoke alarm sounded, their smiles from just playing ball and having fun turned to sour faces of what was to come. The guys would tease them and crack jokes about burnt chicken and dog food. We would stick our finger in our mouths pretending to throw up. The Smith Brothers were also very thin fellas. These are the people, who later in high school became big fans of cafeteria food.

Our little town had some of the toughest moms, too. There were fat moms, skinny ones, short ones, and tall ones. Some of the grandmothers had mini-beards on their chins and weird moles with a single hair sticking out of it on their face. It was like Halloween all year with some of these ladies. Don't get me wrong, they were not all ugly and mean, but enough of them were so that you remembered them clearly.

These older ladies were strong, too, and had big flabby arms that when they got a hold of you . . . it was awful. Some even liked to arm wrestle with you, put you in a headlock, and give you a noogie. A noogie you might ask? A noogie is when one makes a fist and presses the curled middle knuckle of the fingers against your head, twisting and turning until it practically gouges a hole in your head. Where did they learn to do such things?

These ladies ranged in age from young mothers to older women saddled with too many children, many they would have been better off without. In addition to being terrorized daily by their husbands, they had to cope with kids having nothing else to do all summer but routinely get into major trouble. Life without video games and smartphones left us to our own imagination. That often led to an assortment of shenanigans resulting in various levels of mother-empowered punishment.

So, it was more often than not the moms who doled out the day-to-day punishment in our little hamlet. We might misbehave right after dad left for work in the morning or wait until early afternoon after school, but still hours before dad was due home. Dads at work or away from home could not be reached very easily nor did they want to be bothered with news of kids misbehaving. This meant the moms had to formulate plans to deal with managing the behavior of the hooligans when dad was not home.

The moms would get together, plotting, and planning to keep us off our guard. Their eyes were everywhere and they had spies even in our very midst. I only trusted my very best friends and always kept alert for the kid in our gang (yes, we had gangs) with a little more money in his pocket than usual.

The moms had no mercy and no code of honor as they conducted their covert operations. They had stool pigeons, toadies, the Little Old Ladies Broadcasting Network, and a neighborhood of spies to keep watch on us. Still, we managed to evade most of the surveillance and conduct our juvenile operations nonetheless. We were developing critical thinking and guerilla management skills. Now that I think about it, being a kid was a lot like being a grownup. We were preparing ourselves for real life.

Longfellow Elementary School

Chapter 9

Growing Up Small—
More Than Just Words

I attended Longfellow Elementary School from the third through eighth grade. The school was built in 1850 and it probably looked very much the same in 1962 when I started there. Newer composite top desks were mixed in with wooden desks from a previous era. Names, dates, and messages etched into those wooden desks could not be removed. There were nicknames of guys who were by then in their thirties carved into the desktops. This one guy, Spider, was a legend in his own time. He attended the school back in 1955 and must have sat at fifty different desks.

There were big black wall clocks in five or six classrooms that must have been there since the 1940s. The oil soaked wooded floors held the tracks of thousands of students who passed through its halls. And the schoolyard with its gravel playground and secret spots is fresh in my memory.

Many of the classmates I grew up with went on to go to the same high school. That's what I mean by growing up small. Small town, time moving slowly, and things were less complicated. To me, it was a great time to grow up.

Yet, not everything was easy and some of the kids had it harder than others. During this time, some students stayed back to repeat a grade but only a handful dropped out of school. The ones who stayed back had to because they needed to. What I can say is that after completing the eighth grade, most of us could read, write, and knew a little math and science to help get us ready for high school.

Today, big cities push kids through school systems managed by school districts and administrators more concerned with funding and job security than preparing a student for high school and college. I believe many teachers do care, but they can't seem to be able to do their jobs like before. There are too many high school students graduating today who lack the basic skills we once took for granted. Many are not prepared for college, let alone entering a competitive workforce. I agree the smart ones today may be brighter than even some of the best of our class, but I think a higher percentage of the kids in school are now less prepared for the real world than we were.

Another thing that stands out today is the physical size of today's kids. Talk about growing up small, well at least smaller. My apologies to those who may be a little large or overweight, but obesity is a big problem, not only in the United States, but worldwide. There are way too many kids who are overweight today.

In my day, every class had "the fat kid." In a typical class of twenty-five students, there was usually one fat boy and one fat girl. That was it. At most there were two or three. There was not a third or one half of the class, like you see today. The fat kid in my class happened to be a good friend of mine. That was good for me! We called him Fat David—and he was a good sport about it.

Fat David was huge and could easily squash most of us if he could ever catch us. At ten years old I had a sweet tooth but limited financial resources. Fat David was smarter than me. He was good in math and I was lousy. Our friendship was forged using our God-given talents to help fulfill each other's needs—sort of like survival where you pool resources to keep on going.

I, on the one hand, was the local baseball jock and could always get Fat David on my team. So, he got to play ball when otherwise he may have never have had an opportunity on his own. He could hit the smack out of the ball, though. With all that weight behind a mighty swing, he would send balls flying far out into the outfield.

The trouble was, however, he could never get past first base and he was a terrible fielder. We used him at first base and you had to throw the ball directly into his glove or he would not catch it. Fat David helped us develop highly accurate throwing arms. Ground balls, forget about it; they would just roll right by him as he dipped his glove a few inches beneath his waist just to make it look like he was trying.

So, in return for me helping him get to play a little baseball and be part of the team, he helped me with my schoolwork. There was also a bonus in it for me. While I was at his house doing homework, I got to partake in the study-time goodies his mom would bring us. Sodas, cookies, chips, and ice cream would flow as we solved mathematical equations and brushed up on English. Who ever said studying wasn't fun? Fat David was a good guy and I'm glad I was his friend.

Comic Book Ads—Getting Rich

Summer vacation was a time for ditching school books and reading only what we wanted to read, which was pretty much limited to the sports page in the newspaper and our favorite comic books. I remember paying 25 cents for a comic book and laying out in the grass reading about our favorite characters and superheroes. One of the things I loved about those comic books were the advertisements on the back page. There was always a full page of new gadgets like x-ray glasses, joy buzzers, magic tricks, and get rich quick schemes.

I remember this one ad (maybe you do too). It was an ad with this redhead kid smiling and dollar signs floating all around his head. He was surrounded by toys and all kinds of neat stuff he had bought with the money he made from this fantastic business opportunity hawked right there in the comic book. This fair-haired fellow got rich selling seeds! I took one look at this kid and thought, "wow, this is for me!" If this stupid looking kid can make money, why, with my charm, good looks, and connections, I can make a bundle!

So, I filled out a simple order form, mailed it in, and this company shipped me, a little ten-year-old kid, fifty dollars-worth of seeds. There must have been 500 packs of different vegetable and flower seeds. The packages were pretty and professional-looking, but I now know the seed company knew the odds were slim of me ever selling the initial order. I sold two packs to my mother and one pack to my grandma.

When dad got the bill in the mail he was furious. The envelope in the mail had his name on it. You see, we have the same first name and he always picked up the mail on his way home. It's not like I committed fraud or anything. Still, I had to face the consequences of my actions. That meant explaining all of this to my dad.

My dad called the seed company on the phone. After a lot of screaming, yelling, and use of certain threats, my dad got them to agree to take the seeds back. But I had to pay for the parcel post shipping back to the seed company.

Our Underwater Ship

There was also a lot of cool stuff for sale in the back of those old comic books to catch the attention of us kids. There was this one item that caught our eye. It was a fully submersible submarine and it only cost $4.99! I had to have it. The picture showed the submarine floating on top of the water with some kid's head sticking out from the lookout tower at the top. He had a captain's hat on and looked like he was having a great time steering this submarine on top of the water.

I could not handle the $4.99 on my own, so I enlisted the aid of my friend Eddie. We did odd jobs, saved, and pooled our money to send away for this magnificent ship. We made thirty cents here, a quarter here and there, and soon we had enough money to purchase the craft. We told our friends we had purchased a remarkable submarine and bragged about how we would be the only kids with a real underwater ship.

We talked about how we would take it down to the Blackstone River and float for miles, submersing here and there to see fish and the wonders of the river bottom. We waited six weeks for this marvelous craft... and it finally arrived at my house.

It came in a good-sized cardboard box. That was exciting enough and confirmed that this in fact must be a mighty vessel to warrant such a large shipping container. Eddie and I looked at each other with great anticipation, wondering if we had the proper tools to assemble such a craft. We laid the box out on the front porch and fetched an assortment of tools. We then took the pieces out of the shipping box, sorted them, and started to assemble the great craft.

After just a few minutes, we both started crying. Sure, it fit two people, but so did every cardboard refrigerator box. It was painted battleship grey like the picture and came with three lousy stickers, just like the picture in the comic book. It had a cardboard steering wheel you had to put on with tape and even came with one dumb cardboard captain's hat.

We should have gotten the x-ray glasses. At least we would have gotten a good look at Miss Francis, the cute sixth-grade teacher in the tight blouses.

Ten-year-old kids today are too smart to fall prey to such nonsense. They would have Googled "comic book submersible submarine scams" and found about these dashers of dreams right away. The charlatans would have been Yelped to death, sued by the parents, and banished from business. But alas, no Google for us back then.

Dad came home just as we finished putting this piece of garbage together, looked at us and laughed. Dads in the day had no mercy for their son's goof-ups. Even the dog pitched in. He came over to the craft, lifted a leg, and relieved himself on the hull. Yeah, no sympathy, not even from the dog.

With red faces and tears, we cut up the cardboard craft and threw it in the trash. When pestered by our friends, asking if we had received the remarkable submarine, we told them that it was never delivered. We said that the comic book company had returned our money because it was out of stock due to popular demand. After a while, the whole episode was soon forgotten, except for our pride and the $4.99 plus shipping. That was my last comic book merchandise purchase.

CHAPTER 10

The Heist and Other Capers

The Gang and Our Hangouts

We had our little gangs back in our small town in Massachusetts, but they were not like the dangerous city gangs you hear about today. We did not have corner boys selling drugs, didn't wear colors except for an assortment of baseball caps of our favorite team, and no one had tattoos. The only tattoo I ever remember seeing was that of my uncle's little battleship with U.S.N. underneath it. He was in the Navy. We did not do drugs at that age and we claimed no territory other than a few hangouts. We were just groups of youngsters who were told by their parents to "go outside and play!" Imagine that, moms telling their kids to get out of the house to get some exercise and fresh air. I guess she just wanted a little peace and quiet until the old man came home.

Let me give you a little insight into the gangs in my day.

There was an assortment of big kids and little kids belonging to their own group of friends. Sometimes, even a few of the tougher girls would hang out with the guys. That included Jane. You remember Jane. She was six feet tall at the age of twelve, a lefty, and she hit six home runs over the fence in right field the first season she played.

After that first season, some of the coaches (dads) voted to kick her out. I guess they could not have this girl hitting poor Johnny's fastball into orbit every game. So, she hung out with us and was part of our gang. She was the only girl in our little troop, but we stuffed her hair into a dirty baseball cap on her head and no one knew the difference.

We had our special hideouts, a regular group of guys, and this one gal who just hung out together. Hanging out is a lost art. Most ten and eleven-year-old kids today cannot even hang out in their own yard, let alone some place in town. They don't know how to or have anyone to hang out with. They think hanging out means sitting on their butts in someone's house with their hands locked on video game controllers or to smartphone texting the person sitting right next to them. Some are not even allowed to go outside without supervision.

Back then we had our freedom and the confidence of the neighborhood. We always hung out in groups and, you know, there is truth to the fact that there is power in numbers. A bunch of kids with their dogs is not to be messed with. No kid in my old neighborhood was ever kidnapped, molested, or assaulted when we were together and we were not afraid of strangers. Strangers were afraid of us!

Our hangouts were strategically positioned throughout the town. In the center of town, we had what us insiders called *the Intersection*, which included *the Bridge*, our main office, so to speak. The Bridge had various positions of power.

The toughest kid coveted the best vantage point, sitting atop a railing looking down on the others, kind of like how your boss's chair is higher than yours when you meet with him. The next in power stood next to this kid and so on and so on. Across the street was the local combination market and liquor store. This place would soon fall prey to our juvenile ingenuity in overcoming a lack of working capital.

Another establishment was *the Candy Store*, which had a poolroom and card tables in the back where we played high stakes poker. I once won 47 cents. From our corporate location and satellite offices, we planned the events of the day and the capers for the night.

Across from the Bridge was the only fire department in town. Complete with 1940s vintage fire trucks, it was manned by the local volunteers who went down to the station each night after supper. I think these guys just wanted to get away from the wife and kids for a while. They were all blue-collar guys who didn't smile much and certainly did not care for us hanging around right across the street from their shining fire fortress.

In the summer, they would sit out in front of the station on folding chairs. They would glare over at us and we could hear them mumbling together as they smoked their cigarettes and cigars. We could hear them complain about us hanging around smoking our own cigarettes and drinking sodas. They didn't much like us and thought we were just a bunch of juvenile delinquents getting ready to make trouble. We all knew these guys and they knew us, so we had to be careful we didn't offend anyone. I guess they had no place else to go either, so we were not that different. We were all just hanging out.

Hacking Back in the Day

The pool hall was our favorite hangout. It was in the back room of the infamous candy store. Old John was the proprietor and he let us hang out if we spent money. We bought sodas and, yes, he even sold us cigarettes in those days. "They are for my father" was all we had to tell him. We ate chips and junk food, played cards, had the jukebox for music, and we played pool.

Old John had hoped to bring in a little money as well as give us something to do to keep us out of trouble so he brought in a few pay-for-play pool tables. It took one quarter to play a game. Usually, a pool game started with two players who flipped a coin to see who would put in the first quarter. The coin toss winner got to play free. The winner of the first pool game was then challenged by the next guy who had to put up the next quarter, and so on, and so on. The new pool tables worked fine, and for a while generated a little extra income for Old John. But, left to our own devices, namely one skinny-armed kid named Dicky, we figured out how to beat the table fee.

Old John's pool table revenue stream dried up quite a bit once we figured out how to release the balls from inside the pool table without inserting a quarter in the pull slot. That's when we started putting little Dicky Taylor to good use. LD, as we used to call him, had the longest and skinniest arms of anyone I'd even seen. His wrist and hands were small enough to fit inside the narrow slots where the balls came out and slink up and inside the pool table. He was our age, taller but thin (I never ate supper at his house.)

Anyway, LD would slide his skinny arm up under the pool table's quarter coin slot and with his little hand he would reach for the lever way inside the pool table that released the pool balls. LD would charge us a nickel each time he performed his magic and immediately go and buy candy. I guess Old John got something after all, even if it was only five cents. This went on for some time until he finally figured out what was going on and changed the table to something we couldn't hack into. But not to worry, we would utilize LD's talents elsewhere.

Fitting in Small Spaces

Every little town had a corner liquor and convenience store. Beer, cheap wine, and hard liquor were sold right along with newspapers, magazines, cigarettes, and various day-to-day necessities. Now, we weren't old enough to buy alcohol, of course, but we were clever enough to get our hands on it. Enter LD and his skinny appendages.

After closing for the day, the liquor store was a fortress with huge locks on the doors, two-way mirrors, glass alarms, and even a camera pointed at the high-end stuff. The store had a typical New England stone-walled basement where all the cases of beer, liquor, and extra goodies were kept. It was nice and cool down there, making it a great wine cellar. The basement was part of an old foundation and had only one small window in the back of the store. Oddly, there were no lights in the backyard of the store. The small window had two iron bars so that nobody could just pull back the glass frame covering the window and climb in. The space measured about eighteen-inches high and three feet across. The two bars came straight down about twelve inches apart.

Late one night, after the store closed and it was dark outside, a couple of us guys and LD headed out for the liquor store. We had two or three lookouts that would light a cigarette to warn us if someone was approaching. There would be one or two other guys to help carry the contraband, and naturally, LD to carry out the plan. It took about fifteen minutes or so for him to put in his arms and twist his body to manipulate himself through the iron window bars and down into the storage basement. It was hilarious—it was like we were watching a circus act.

Here is this skinny kid contorting himself like a rubber man through the window bars and into the store. Once through the bars and window, LD was smack dab in the middle of a king's ransom of assorted forbidden beverages and goodies. We didn't take too much at any one time and only enough for our little group of bandits. We didn't want to raise suspicion, you know, and there's only so much a kid can carry. Just a six-pack or so and some treats for the night. We must have been fourteen or so at the time, so one beer was more than enough for any of us. Sometimes we did not even open any of the beer for days. We would just walk around with them hanging out of our pocket, trying to look cool and tough.

LD did not even have to crawl back out the window to leave. There was a big wooden door in the back of the basement with the handle only on the inside and it locked automatically when it was closed. They didn't want anybody opening it from the outside but they didn't seem concerned about someone opening it from the inside. This went on for a while until Dickey got too big to fit through the bars. All good things come to an end.

The Candy Store Heist

Now if you thought stealing a few cans of beer using our skinny friend was something, you will appreciate this next story. And I guarantee every kid involved can still recall this ingenious operation with fondness, if not with a little shame as well. It cannot be denied, these events happened and the participants, of which there were many, would surely recall the parts they played. I am certain a sly smirk would appear on their face and I would love to be able to share a beer with them recollecting these stories.

This will be one of the longer little stories, but I think it is important to tell it in its full, unadulterated, and shameful glory.

First I need to give you the layout of the candy store, our objectives, methods, and the participants. Does this not sound like the prelude to a new movie? Well, the candy store was located on our not-so-busy Main Street. It was our go-to place for everything a kid could need back then: candy, comic books, sodas, and whatever we needed on a warm summer's day. They also made a great ice cream cone. You got a single scoop for 15 cents, a double for a quarter and if you were hungry and had 35 cents, a triple scoop was as good as it gets.

It all started one day when I noticed that whenever I ordered an ice cream cone, the old fat lady behind the counter went through the same ritual in making every ice cream cone. First, she would make us pay (you can't trust these little tykes you know). After collecting our money, she would open the cash draw and put the money into the appropriate coin slot in the old key register. As with today's cash registers this was a place for pennies, nickels, dimes, and quarters.

Her foil was that she would leave the cash register draw open. Why I don't know, but it was to be her demise. After putting our money into the cash draw she would waddle, yes truly waddle, around the counter to open the lid on the waist-high freezer that held the cold ice cream containers down below inside the freezer. Each ice cream flavor was stored in round corrugated open containers. The freezer was very cold and it took a good deal of effort to scoop out the hard ice cream. The old lady would have to bend her rotund body way down inside the freezer, practically disappearing into the depths of the ice cream freezer, taking almost her whole head, arm, and hand to scoop the ice cream portions to make a cone. She always had to gasp for air on the way back up as she added the scoop to the cone.

The poor woman tired easily and always gave us a snooty look as if we were making her work too hard. We always ordered double or triple scoops for this scam so that she would have to go down inside the freezer two or three times for each cone. And we would order two, three, or maybe four cones at a time.

I noticed that when she had two or three transactions in a row, she would collect the first sale, but then leave the cash drawer open for the second sale so that she would not have to ring it up again. I guess she did not want to create more work for herself, or maybe she was tapping into Old John's till. Anyway, her ice cream making routine provided the opportunity to hatch a most ingenious plan. Are you starting to get the picture?

So, a few friends and I talked about how we could take advantage of the open cash register draw. It was right there, ripe for the taking: Nickels, dimes, and quarters just waiting to be snatched up. But how were we going to get them and not get caught? We calculated the risks and developed a foolproof plan. Kind of like a business plan.

The objective was to have one kid stand as close to the cash register as possible, extend his arm as far as he could, and reach around the table corner into the cash drawer with his fingers lifting as many coins as possible. He would do this while the old lady's head was down in the freezer making an ice cream cone for an accomplice. Now, to pull this off, we needed five or six guys, various visual and sound effects for distractions, and a ruthless gang to orchestrate and carry out the mission.

The cast included two or three kids buying ice cream cones with money in hand. Then, we had the rest of the team, the A-Team so to speak. There was *Potato Chip Bag Rustler Guy*. His job was to go to the potato chip section and make believe he was searching through the bags for his favorite chips. He had to rustle the bags making enough noise so that the old lady could not hear the coins being rifled from the open cash draw.

The coin lifter was none other than Little Dicky, of course. This guy must have been a carnival performer in a previous life. With his long arms and skinny fingers probing, snaking around corners and into the cash draw coin slots, he grabbed as many coins as he could each time the poor old lady descended into the depths of the ice cream freezer box. The first try at this was a really close call and she almost caught us.

We needed more noise and distractions so we brought in *Soda Bottle Guy*, an accomplice who came in with empty soda bottles just at the right time, clanking and clunking the bottles making even more noise. It was a symphony of petty larceny. The store gave us two cents for each clean, unbroken bottle we returned and I think the store got like five cents back so we were getting screwed anyway.

We sometimes brought in *Allergy Guy*. We made this one kid smell an onion for a few minutes before walking into the candy store. His job was to cough, sneeze, and cry, creating even more noise.

Of course, the key man was LD. He would stand next to the counter pretending he was next one in line to buy an ice cream cone. With an innocent smile on his face, his long skinny arms and fingers snaked down, up and around the counter into the cash drawer. It was like a cold serpent slithering around the cashbox stalking its silver prey.

I was *Lookout Guy*, the one standing outside the store's front door ready to burst in and create chaos if I thought anyone was about to enter the store. It was never very busy, though, and we always did this mid-afternoon when most of town was asleep.

The heist was usually good for two or three quarters, a few nickels, and dimes. Once satisfied with enough coins, we would meet out at the WWII Park and split up the booty. Now, we did this at least once each day all summer long and never got caught. Really—never caught. But we did reinvest the funds back into the store. Kind of like a CD, only we did not need the principle. We took our ill-gotten proceeds and went back to the candy store to play pool and buy sodas and candy using poor Old John's own money. It was our version of the *velocity of money*. You can Google the term. Well, at least we kept it in town.

Many years later when I came back to visit the little town I was raised in, I walked the streets trying to visualize the places we used to frequent and recall all the crazy things we'd done. I can still see the face of the old lady in the candy store, the teenage card sharks and pool hustlers, and the grumpy volunteer fireman staring at us. It was as if they had never left and their spirits were still there, lingering and haunting my memories. I feel their faces upon me now. I feel their presence and hear them say "we know who you are and what you did..." It was such a long time ago, but it was so much fun.

The Pay Phone Caper

Talk about being in the right place at the right time. I think God teases me at times just to make sure I still believe in miracles. Miracle or not, I was fortunate to benefit from one of His mighty tools. Lightning!

Right next to the liquor store across the street from our bridge headquarters was an outside pay phone, the only pay phone on our side of town. It was a glass-sided booth with doors that folded open and closed. The phone was black with a finger dial faceplate and a hand receiver that was always getting smashed against its metal base and a coin slot that was damaged but not broken from numerous attempts to get the money out. Gosh they made things strong back then. The coin box was an impenetrable steel fortress and the phone itself was made of indestructible plastic. No matter how hard someone slammed the phone against anything, nothing could break it. We were never able to break into the coin box. It just sat there teasing us, mocking us with its silver treasure of nickels, dimes, and quarters.

One day there was this big, loud thunderstorm. It was typical New England storm weather and we scattered from our hangout. Rain was hailing down and the sky turned an awful gray with streaks of black. As I ran to my bike, I saw a bolt of lightning hit the pay phone nearby. There was a big zapping noise and smoke was coming out of the top of the thing. I thought for sure that the pay phone had made its final call.

After the rain ended and the skies cleared, I did not pay much attention to the pay phone. It looked like it had survived the storm and I didn't think anything more of the lightning striking it. But a funny thing happened later in the day.

Now, lots of people used this pay phone every day. There were no cell phones back then and pay phones were very useful. There was always a salesman who had to call his office or a customer, or some guy calling his girlfriend. I guess the pay phone was a good business investment for somebody and generated cash for whoever rented it out or owned it.

But they would soon discover a decline in revenues, a change in their sales trend, so to speak. You see, I was privy to the phenomenon resulting from that lightning strike. Every time someone used the pay phone, they naturally inserted the required amount of coins for the call and kept adding in coins to continue talking. Some of these bag-draggers (salesmen) and Romeos could talk forever, so quite a bit of coinage was going in there.

That afternoon after the lightning strike, I was hanging by

myself on the Bridge. A car pulled up to the pay phone, a guy got out and he started talking on the phone. He finished his call, got in his car and took off. A few minutes after he had left, the pay phone started ringing. No one was around to answer it. Who answers a pay phone, anyway? After four or five rings, the phone makes a different ringing noise and I heard what sounds like coins falling into the coin box.

Don't you know it, the money that the previous caller had deposited dropped back into the change return slot. Naturally this caught my attention. Remember, I was the only one hanging out on the Bridge when this happened. I alone had witnessed all of this pay phone commotion and asked myself, "Is this really happening?"

I looked around to make sure no one was watching me or had heard what had just occurred. I crossed the street, moseyed over to the pay phone and stuck my fingers into the change return slot. Lo and behold, a nice stash of change was in there! Three or four dimes, a few nickels, and even a quarter. Must have been at least fifty cents there for the taking. I looked around again to make sure no one was looking, took out the coins and put them in my pocket.

Evidently, the lightning striking the pay phone had altered some of the electronics and was returning anything that was deposited, but only after four or five minutes after the caller had hung up the phone.

This was indeed a window of opportunity that required around the clock surveillance. I could not possibly monitor the Bridge position by myself all day, every day, and I could not hope to keep this secret. So, I enlisted the help of a few trusted buddies to help watch my investment, I mean the phone, and share in the proceeds. Soon, we had a small crew of fellas who would take turns at different hours to monitor the pay phone.

The Bridge was a popular hangout spot anyway so no one thought it odd kids were there in the first place. The first day we made about five dollars, the second day even more. And soon we had too much money; well, more than any ten-year-old kid in 1965 should have had in his pocket during summer vacation. We bought candy and soda for our friends, the latest comic books, and even some new baseballs. There was no end to our new-found revenue stream. I think the guy who was supposed to check the pay phone took a few weeks off for summer vacation, which was bad for him, good for us.

But, all good things do eventually come to an end. After about three weeks, we finally saw the guy who came to check on the pay phone. We knew it was the collector guy and not somebody who wanted to make a call. He shows up with a bunch of keys, I guess for other pay phones, and he opened the lock box. Naturally, there was nothing in it. I and a few of the guys were hanging out on the Bridge, just hanging out not causing any trouble, but leery of this guy coming to get ours, I mean, his cash.

He opened the cash box and all we could hear was a bunch of cuss words and then he gave us a stare that could freeze hell. We could not help but to start to snicker, which led to out all out laughing at the look of surprise on this guy's face. He then knew that we knew. But, there was nothing he could do about it. Our guys stuck together like glue, no rats on the Bridge.

The very next day another guy came and replaced the pay phone with a new one. The phone was back to normal and our cash flow back to zero, at least for a little while. But I can say, whenever there was a lightning storm, us kids would rush to the pay phone!

Train trestle

CHAPTER 11

Ghostbusters

Dirty Dave's House

In the summer of 1965, my friends and I did more and ventured further than most eleven-year-olds could ever imagine today. We roamed for miles on our banana seat steeds of steel with our loyal and protective canine buddies. We frequented junkyards where ferocious mutts strolled the grounds ready to bite our heads off should we have dared to enter their domain.

We jumped on slow moving trains for quick rides to the next little town and then back again to come home. These trains would stop by certain areas to hook up to other cars, so it was easy to hop on and hook a ride. Still, there was a slight air of danger to it all and we often got a little scrape here and there during these journeys, especially when hopping off.

We went swimming in deep quarries and lonely ponds in the wood with snakes swimming around in the water close by. We hung from train trestles while the train went by overhead. We drove old cars around fields, sometimes holding our own demolition derby if there was more than one old clunker. We got dirty, sometimes bloodied, and at the end of each day you could tell we had a good day. We slept like babies every night.

Yes, we were legends in our time. Well, at least in our own minds. We were brave and daring for a bunch of youngsters.

There was this one time, when we had quite an experience at an old abandoned house in a secluded part of town. Most folks called it Dirty Dave's House. Everybody knew about the old house, the weird stories of how it was haunted, and of the strange things that happen there. It was very old, abandoned long before, and Dave himself had died in the house along with his menagerie of assorted pets—more like crazed animals, from the stories we heard.

In the city, this house would have been torn down long before. The clapboards, once painted green, were peeling, adding a creepy appearance to the dilapidated structure. Rusted gutters and crumbling wooden stairs leading up to the porch enhanced the creepiness. The front door hung by one hinge and creaked with the wind. It was a relic of a house rotting away, one that nobody cared about. Most folks hoped it would just burn down one day. But it was still in Dave's family and they were hanging on to it in hopes of better days.

There were long-standing challenges among our small rival gangs and this house was one of them. The dare involved venturing into Dirty Dave's house on a moonless night, walking first through the front door and through the entire house, and exiting out the back door—preferably still alive.

The challenged gangs met just outside of the old house in front of the broken front gate during the day. Two or three of the bravest kids volunteered to enter the evil dwelling and agreed upon a night to do it. The date was set. It would be the upcoming Saturday night because that was when we were supposed to be camping in the backyard of one our buddies. It was also a new moon, so the night would be black.

For our parent's sake, my buddies and I played up the camping ruse to perfection. We waited until it was dark outside and our parents thought we were in our sleeping bags inside the tent. Then the ghostbuster crew prepared for the night ahead: Flashlights, check; slingshots, check. When all was quiet and we were certain it was safe to venture out, we went off into the night like little gremlins. Bicycle shadows dancing tall in the darkness, we were off to Dirty Dave's for the adventure that lay ahead.

It was rumored that Dave died sitting in a chair in one of the rooms with his mangy dog, Old Red, sitting in his lap. The old men in town told us that Red was a nasty dog, never brushed or washed, much like Dave; hence the nickname. They also said that the only thing Dave ever fed poor Red were rats he caught in traps. And then there was the rumor that Old Red once attacked a paperboy and bit his leg off at the knee. We are not talking Lassie here.

When we went inside the house during the daytime it was okay because it was light out and it was just an interesting old place full of ancient yellowed newspapers, assorted junk strewn about, and ripped filthy furniture covered with cobwebs. There was also a lot of broken glass all over the place from guys throwing rocks through the windows. There were still some pictures of weird looking people hanging crookedly on the walls, the photos all a brownish tint. They wore clothes that did not fit very well and no one was smiling, all having rather dazed looks on their faces. Didn't anyone ever smile back then?

There was a foul odor in the house and there was this one spot on the floor where animal bones and fur were fused into the wood floor. We always thought these were the remains of Old Red and that the soiled clothing lying in the big chair was the last of Dirty Dave as well. This was all creepy stuff for ten- and eleven-year-old kids.

Saturday night came and it was time to carry out the dare or forever be cast as the cowards of Main Street. We rode our bikes to the house and laid them down at the end of the long dirt driveway. There were no streetlights, only a slight outline of the new moon. We told our dogs to sit and stay with the bikes. Not only did they sit as commanded, but quickly lay down and went to sleep.

The three of us ventured into the old house in order to preserve our honor and make history. It had to be around ten o'clock and was so dark that our small Boy Scout flashlights were barely able to light the way and we could barely see beyond our noses.

The challenge was that we had to take one of the old photos from the wall and take it back to the camp in order to show the other guys how brave we were. So, off we went. We entered the old house one at a time, armed with our flashlights and a stick to fend off Old Red should he spring out and try to eat us. The floor creaked with every step, an owl hooted somewhere in one of the rooms, and we heard what must have been rats rustling on the floor amidst the junk. Every little noise seemed amplified about ten times over. We were surrounded by evil. This was way before the *Ghostbusters* movies or the paranormal stuff you see on television these days, but we had our imaginations.

We entered the room where we had been told Old Red lay waiting to be resurrected from the pile of fur and bones. Our spotlights fell upon the torn fabric chair where Dirty Dave died, leaving only a soiled red flannel shirt, faded jeans, and one old shoe. Suddenly, a rotting floorboard broke and Johnny Bray's leg went halfway down into the floor. He screamed in pain, we screamed in fear. I fell face first right in front of the pile of bones and fur.

Now, I not only saw bones and fur, but I imagined giant teeth grinning right at me as well. It was Old Red's teeth getting ready to chomp me right in the face. We dropped our flashlights and started running every which way. Mikey O'Leary ran right into the big chair with the soiled old clothes and fell into the soiled seat cushion. He got tangled in the old clothes and the old flannel shirt hung on to him as he was running. The more he ran, the more that old soiled shirt wrapped around his body. He stumbled out of the house and fell on the ground. We found the flannel shirt in the driveway. Surely Dirty Dave had tried to nab him and was going to strangle him with his old shirt.

As I was running through the dark house, I fell and my pants got caught on a nail sticking out of the floor. Only, at the time, I didn't know it was a nail that had ripped my pants and scratched my leg. To me, at that moment, it was Old Red that had gotten me and torn my pants with his teeth and bit my leg.

Finally, Mikey and I escaped from the house of horrors and into the junk filled, weed infested front yard. We were crying and scared. But where was Johnny Bray? We realized he was still inside as we could hear him crying and yelling for help. He was trapped in the broken floorboards. We had to do something. We tried to calm ourselves down and waited for a few minutes, but we knew we had to save Johnny. We noted that Dirty Dave and his dog were nowhere in sight and we were safe, away from the house. But what about Johnny? What if Old Red went back in to eat him?

Mikey stayed in the driveway and I went to Johnny's house to tell his dad what had happened. Now you realize, it was rather late at night and Johnny's mom and dad were in bed. I banged on the front door and Johnny's dad opened it. I was out of breath, talking in circles, but he could see my ripped pants with blood dripping down my leg. I think I told him that Old Red had eaten Johnny or maybe Dirty Dave had killed him. He calmed me down enough so that I could tell him what had happened. I took him back to Dirty Dave's house and Mr. Bray rescued Johnny from his floorboard prison. Except for a few scrapes and maybe soiled underwear, he was fine.

We ended up staying the night at Johnny's house. His mom cleaned us up and gave us something to eat. His dad asked us if we wanted to stay up and watch TV. He said there was a good monster movie coming on. We passed and went to bed.

Early the next morning, we went back to the little campsite outside my house, packed up our things, and my friends went home. Mr. and Mrs. Bray never did say a word to our parents. Not that we ever knew about, anyway. Parents are hard to understand when you're ten years old. It could have been a lot worse, but it was something that bonded the three of us for a long time. We never did get that old photograph, but boy did the gang enjoy our story!

Train trestle

Chapter 12

Death Defying

The Train Trestle

How many parents today would have let their ten-year-old boys out for the afternoon alone roaming the entire town? Saturday was our day to escape from school, the scrutiny of parents, and taunts of older siblings. My friends and I hung out at several places in the little town, many of which we had been warned to stay away from. The train trestle was one of those places. It was dangerous, and looking back I'm amazed no one ever got killed doing the stupid things we did.

Bums and vagrants gathered underneath the train trestle on the banks of the river and the whole place just screamed trouble. That did not matter to us, though. The trestle was a place where us guys challenged each to death defying feats of foolishness and where legends were built.

Our bicycles were our locomotives and our imagination wild

enough to bring out some of the most creative cycling games ever invented. These should have been events for the Olympics.

One game we played was called *biking-the-rail*. It was a simple but daring competition. You put your bike on the train track and tried to keep both wheels on the track to see how far you could pedal before falling off the track. Simple enough, huh? Sure, on firm ground it's a snap and so what if you fall off, a few cuts and bruises, just like camping.

But we had to make it a little more challenging by seeing who could ride the three-inch wide rail the furthest across the trestle. You see, beneath the trestle ran the Blackstone River, a swampy, goopy flow of something that at one time was water. The river spewed with toxics from the local textile and glass factories. This was before the EPA and clean water conservation programs. It wasn't that deep, but if you fell in it, you would surely turn into one of the toxic swamp creatures we saw at the movies.

To take it a step further, we sometimes even waited for the train to approach the trestle. We would have a lookout about a half a mile down the tracks to wave a red cloth tied on a stick to tell us when a train was approaching. Sometimes we'd have to wait hours for a train, but it was worth it. We only lost one bicycle in all our years of doing this.

Timmy Mac had a fast bike and he was the best at riding the rails. But there was one day that was not to be his day. We saw the red flag that signaled a train was approaching the trestle. Timmy jumped on his steed of steel and began riding swiftly with great balance and skill. He was going along smoothly, the tires of the bike sticking to the rails like they were glued on. Suddenly, he lost control of the bike and went tumbling off to one side of the tracks.

If you ever have seen train tracks, they are laid on and bordered by small granite rocks angling downward on each side.

He was scraped from the rocks, but lucky to be close to the end of the trestle and scampered to safe ground way ahead of the train. Unfortunately, his bicycle had fallen inside the train tracks. Now, big freight trains don't stop very quickly and in fact, this train did not even try to stop at all. Even though it was going very slowly, it did not slow down. We had tortured these train conductors throughout the years with our antics on the trestle and I swear I could see the conductor laughing as his engine roared over the tracks and, of course, the fallen Schwinn.

Sparks flew from the train undercarriage and its huge steel wheels and the sound of crunching metal was terrifying. I know all the bums were having a good time at our expense. Timmy's bike was a really cool 20-inch fastback with big tires, raised handlebars, and a banana seat. After the train passed, you could not tell what it was.

Obviously, this was the end of our days at the trestle. Our parents found out what we had been doing and what had happened as we all got letters from the train company threatening to send the police to our houses. Looking back, we all realized how lucky it was that Timmy was not hurt badly or even killed that day. But, we chalked up another memory and rite of passage in a long line of passages yet to come.

The Old Junk Yard

I'm skipping a few years here, moving ahead to when we were a little older, maybe fifteen or so. Even though we weren't old enough to legally drive an automobile, we used to pool our money together and buy clunkers from one of the old guys in town. There was never a bill of sale, title, or license plate that came with these old cars. We got nothing in writing to tie either party to the car.

Twenty or thirty bucks cold cash could get you the keys to old man Weston's 1952 black Chevy sedan or any number of the old rust buckets hanging around in his field. He lived close by, up on a hilly field by the river, so it was easy to push the car downhill to a spot where we could get it running with the gas we had siphoned off from some unsuspecting neighbor's car. Not many locking gas caps back then.

Anyway, we would drive this old beater around in a big field, running over rocks and ruts, bouncing up and down while taking turns at the wheel. These old cars had a clutch with a stick shift on the steering column. The seats were often worn away, the clutches were semi-frozen and you had these huge steering wheels. That made it difficult for one person to push in the clutch and shift gears at the same time. So, one kid would push in the clutch and the other kid shift and steer the car.

The cars were usually so run down by the time we got them, they barely reached twenty miles per hour. When the car finally took its last breath, we would dump it over a cliff into the Blackstone River. There must be at least ten cars at the bottom of that cliff by now, sunken onto the riverbed. And except for a few scratches, we never got hurt.

There were times when we would need to fix up the car a little to get it running. Back then almost all car parts were interchangeable. And there were only a few major car brands, Ford, Chevy, and Pontiac being the most popular. The carburetors, distributor caps, alternators, generators, etc., fit each make of car. Even radios, heaters and important parts could be installed in different models. The problem was getting these parts so that we could at least get the old cars running again. But auto parts cost money and we had little of that left after paying for the clunker.

Enter Wally, another in a line of what I'll call *useful friends*. Useful friends have something you need or want. I had many good friends, but most were not very useful. Wally's dad was a veterinarian. We used to watch him put our dogs, cats, and other animals to sleep with anesthesia so that he could operate on them to help make them well again. What a wonderful drug, the animal goes to sleep, is fixed up, and then wakes up safe and sound.

Now, we knew there was a treasure trove of automobile parts at Kringley's Auto Salvage at the far end of town. He had what seemed to us to be thousands of wrecked cars lying around from which he sold parts. Old Kringley also had several mean looking junkyard dogs that he only fed old hubcaps and rusted bolts. The salvage yard was protected by a six-foot high chain link fence, but that fence was more for show than effect. Compared to the awful fate should we have met up with any of the junkyard monsters, the fence was not our biggest concern. Those beasts would surely have torn us from limb to limb if we had tried to jump the fence to get inside the junkyard.

I don't remember whose idea it was, but one of us schemed up the plan to inject a few pounds of hamburger with the animal anesthesia. We tried it one Friday night and the plan worked to perfection. After it had closed for the evening, we went over to the junkyard and started shaking the fence. We made a lot of noise and sure enough, out came six or seven of the dogs with mouths foaming and teeth snarling as they tried to gnaw through the metal fence to kill us. Our hearts pounding, we turned and ran in utter fear, but not before tossing a bag filled with the concoction-soaked hamburger over the fence. We heard the dogs battling each other each to get a piece of their fair share of the hamburger.

As the dogs enjoyed their feast, we hung out close by to the fence, but not too close. Soon, there was no sound, no barking or snarling sounds of death. It took less than fifteen minutes, but one-by-one each of the bloodthirsty creatures began to wobble, stagger, and eventually lay down and went to sleep. We thought we'd killed them, but we checked and could see they were still breathing. Their menacing expressions disappeared, replaced by a peaceful, almost Golden Retriever-like smile. I think they were dreaming of hamburgers.

We jumped the fence, went about our larcenous intentions quickly and efficiently, gathering as many of the parts we needed to fix the car as we could find.

From time to time after that, we'd go back to the junkyard to buy some cheaper parts and ask if he had something we'd taken. He'd say "Yes," and go look for it, but come back shortly shaking his head telling us he must have sold it. We'd say, "Oh, shucks," and as we left, look at each other with devilish smiles, knowing all well that the carburetor or some other part we had taken was sitting in the old Chevy, along with a whole bunch of other parts from the old man. Poor old Kringley never knew what hit him.

We eventually acquired some semblance of a conscience and stopped raiding the place. I think we started feeling bad for the dogs. They were getting used to seeing us with the hamburger deliveries and started to greet us like little puppies. When we would come to the salvage yard during business hours, they stopped growling at us. They would whimper and drool, expecting more of the tasty hamburger. Beats hubcaps and rusted bolts. Mr. Kringley was amazed at how the dogs did not growl at us. I think he figured out that we had pulled off something.

CHAPTER 13

Come Play

Playgrounds

Recently, I made a point to ride around the town I now call home to check out the beautiful elementary schools in the neighborhood. School had been out for about a month and I thought I would see a lot of activities happening on the fields and playgrounds. I noticed that most schools had gleaming playground areas with colorful play equipment. The ball fields and soccer fields were well maintained and beckoning for use. What I also noticed was that there was no one around. Oh, the places were spotless but if the playgrounds could talk, they would be saying, "Please, kids, come play."

Alas, the playground's plea for companionship and use of the facilities went unanswered. Maybe it was because it lacked some of the appeal of the playground in my day. You know, stuff like broken glass and challenging play equipment you risked life and limb to climb and spin on.

I remember the merry-go-round where ten kids would spin around until we were so dizzy we either fell off or jumped off to throw up. And there was the seesaw, an engineering marvel if I ever did see one. This diabolical device was designed to either catapult a trusting friend into space or drop him like a rock from the top position. Many a mezzo-soprano was born on the seesaw. Monkey bars, well, should have been just for monkeys. This was an array of bars designed for twisting and climbing, hanging from your arms, feet, and legs. Everyone my age has fallen from these bars and hit the ground hard at some time in their childhood.

I think the playground gave us a physical workout and helped make us tough. No one I ever knew got killed at the playground or suffered any major trauma. Scurrying around town in old torn blue jeans, along with a few scrapes, cuts, and bruises told everyone you were having a good time. And they knew you had a good day by the stains on your shirt. Aside from a little playground blood, the stains might be some ketchup and mustard on your arm sleeves, which meant you had eaten a great hotdog at the local drive-in. Life's pleasures were not measured by clean clothes.

Playing Hill Dill in the School Yard

I'm not sure if anyone outside of Millville, Massachusetts has ever heard of this schoolyard game, but a recent Fox News segment by Bill O'Reilly reminded me of it. Hill Dill was a game we played almost every recess during my elementary school years. It was played in a section of the schoolyard comprised of rock and gravel where many a pants leg was torn and knee scraped.

The game started with one person volunteering to be the Hill Diller. He was one against many lined up against a fence at one end of the schoolyard. We learned about the Battle of Thermopylae in 480 B.C. in which King Leonidas and 300 Spartans defended themselves from a Persian invasion against overwhelming odds. Way before the movie came out, we had our own reenactment where we relived the epic every recess at noon.

The objective of the Hill Diller was to tag as many runners as he could before they reached the other end of the yard. It was a straight line to the other side, but you had to weave your way around to dodge the Hill Diller. If he caught you, then you would have to help him tag runners during the next charge. Now, because this was more of a running at full steam contact game, the tagging was more of a pushing down of the runners than tagging them, resulting in torn pants and bruised appendages.

None of the games we played were totally safe. No "tag and you're it" and then take a drink from a sippy cup. You got tagged by being pushed down and then enslaved to help the guy who just pushed you down. This progression of runs and tagged runners resulted in more and more bruised and battered Hill-Dillers pitted against less and less runners until there is only one sole person left at the very end. It usually ended up in a gang beating of the last runner, but every now and then a legend would be born of the guy who eluded twenty or so classmates and got to the other end without being tagged. I never could make it to the end, usually giving up early in the game in order to save on clothes, Band-Aids, and stitches.

My Bill O'Reilly reference regards the abolishment by today's guardians of youth in schools where such violent games as tag and dodge ball are banned. God forbid we let our children take part in such violent and dangerous activities.

Imagine today's kids being tagged and called *it*. "Your IT!" That would suck to be *it*. You know, I survived, as did most all my classmates. I was *it* many times. I liked being *it*. Just another rite of passage kids today will never know. They will miss out on being *it* and with it an important life-lesson like what it means to get knocked down, dust oneself off, and get back into the fray. After all, isn't that what life is all about? Live, learn, get better or get the hell out.

Not everyone got a trophy the first time out when I grew up. You earned it, cherished it, and were proud of what you accomplished. Like I said before, these are foregone times, but they are not forgotten.

The Older Guy – Bobby B.

I think Bobby B. was around twenty-two years old when he returned from Vietnam. I remembered Bobby as one of the older guys who never cut us much slack. He did not harass us too much or make us feel like little shitholes like most of the other big guys, but I guess he too had to play the tough guy role just like the other big guys.

In his youth, Bobby attained Eagle Scout, was a good sportsman, and an otherwise good guy who went off to fight for his country back in 1966. He came back a different person. In 1969 I was fifteen years old, impressionable, and looking for someone else other than my dysfunctional dad to look up to. Bobby, in his own way, provided me with some things every young guy needs.

In those days, no one would even have thought that some older guy hanging out with kids a little younger than themselves to be a pervert or a threat to their wellbeing. Instead Bobby acted as a big brother role model, something most of us lacked. He knew how to do a lot of cool things and taught us some interesting lessons. He showed us what to look out for and how to take care of ourselves. Bobby B. was our friend.

When I think of him, I feel lucky to have known him. Here was this Vietnam era war veteran hanging out with us guys. The biggest fight we ever got in was swinging our fists wildly with our eyes shut while wrestling each other to the ground. Each time, our minor battles produced no more than few scratches or at worse a black eye. Little did we realize what this young man had been through and the life and death battles he faced daily in a far-off land.

I recall this one particular day when we were going camping with Bobby. He asked me to go back into his room and look for his compass in his top drawer, as he was going to teach us how to read the compass in the woods. When I got to his room and opened the drawer to his desk, I pushed a few things around and found the compass, but I also noticed a small box with a United States Army insignia. Being a nosey kid, I opened the box and found two medals with colorful ribbons. One was a Purple Heart and the other had words that said TET Offensive. I never asked Bobby about them but I later learned what they meant and stood for.

I think of that young guy fighting for his life firing his rifle at other young men fighting for their lives and their country. How scared and confused he must have been. I was lucky enough not to have to go through that. Bobby died in 1985 from cancer. He never smoked cigarettes and always stayed in good shape. Later, I learned of Agent Orange and how that was used in Vietnam to defoliate the forest.

When I read of his death, I thought of the great times we had camping, fishing, and telling ghost stories by lantern light. I don't think he ever married and may have become a recluse living in the wilderness somewhere in Maine, enjoying the outdoors and just being himself. Real friendships are far and few between and we should cherish them.

Hey, It was the Sixties— Brownies for the Math Teacher

I remember it was the eighth grade. Our math teacher, I'll call him Mr. Kennedy, was a nice little guy of about five foot two or so, and he drove a funny little car. Most of the kids, including the girls, were all taller than he was and we used to always make trouble for him. One day, this girl, I'll call her Laurie, brought in some brownies. As you can imagine, these were *special* brownies her older sister had baked the night before. They had been meant for her and her friends for an upcoming weekend party. Hey, it was the Sixties, man.

Anyway, Laurie decided to bring in a few of the special brownies to school that day and offered one to Mr. Kennedy just as the lunch period ended and math class was about to begin. The lesson started off okay, but it took only about ten minutes before the brownie kicked in for Mr. Kennedy. Solving x was about to take on a whole new dimension.

Most of the class was in on the ruse. Right in the middle of writing out a problem on the chalkboard, Mr. Kennedy stopped for what seemed like ten minutes without turning around. I thought I heard him giggle a little, and then he turned to face the class and told us to take a fifteen-minute break. He left some geek in charge while he took a little time to compose himself. A couple of the bully guys eventually stuffed the geek into a trash can and we all left the room at the end of class as if nothing had ever happened. Mr. Kennedy didn't come back that day.

The fact was, we had a tough class the next period and did not want to make any waves, so we just acted as if nothing had ever happened. The next day, Mr. Kennedy was back in school and everything appears to be normal. We had our math class, but right at the end he gives us a special problem to solve. It was a hoot, something about how pharmacology and math can be intertwined.

St. Augustines Church

CHAPTER 14

The Smoking Can Show

Going to Catholic Church

Alas, religion has had good and bad effects on me. I don't know how to handle it to this day, especially Catholicism. But I am kind of an expert here. You see, my sister was a nun who left the convent and later married a former priest. You can't make this stuff up.

So, my family tried to raise me to be a good little Italian Catholic boy and tried to make me go to church on Sunday. I even made it a few times. See, they did not go very often themselves, but I was expected to go every week; typical of parents back then. They preached to you, but did not practice what they preached.

Aside from taking up valuable playtime on a Sunday morning, I found our Catholic church a strange and scary place. Our church was a huge old wooden structure built in the 1800s. It had tall ceilings, lots of statutes, and multi-colored stained glass windows that when sunlight hit them, gave off an eerie light.

Among the many strange noises in that old church was an old creaking floor, plus the booming echoes of people coughing and whispering to each other. And God forbid if anybody dropped something on the floor; it sounded like a bomb went off. To a little kid, the place sounded more like the Creeper's Crypt than a church. It had a weird smell as well. I guess anything over 150 years old will smell bad. My grandpa was only ninety and he did not smell very good, either.

Well, if I happened to make it into the church, we had to sit down on a hard, wooden seat in the pews. The seats were so low, as little kids, we could hardly see over the tall seatbacks in front of us. We were trapped inside this huge wooden galley for an entire hour, listening to Latin gibberish and trying to keep still. We tried to be quiet and not make any noise that might attract the attention of the guard nuns who roamed the aisles with their arsenal of torture tools.

These guard nuns, dressed in long black dresses with white headbands and funny hats carried with them long sticks. These spear-like sticks were armed with pointy, hard rubber bullet-like tips on the end of them. Out of nowhere, some five-foot tall guard nun would stick you in the back right between the shoulder blades if you were talking or fidgeting. They also had a big coil of rosary beads with a big iron cross. You did not want to get whacked by that thing. The guard nuns were well armed and it was best you did not screw with them.

And finally, topping off this hour of kid-misery was the creepy sunlight glimmering through the stain glass windows and the super loud pipe organ music. It was like being trapped inside a wizard's crystal ball.

The Catholic Mass is a ritual of repetition. I could never figure it out. Do it once, then it's over, waiter I'll take my check now. Experience something else for Heaven's sake. People have been doing this same thing for hundreds of years. In my opinion, it's a ridiculous routine of unnecessary regimen and drills to satisfy a man-made ritual. The first time I was exposed to this spectacle I thought it was part of a Catholic exercise class or they were preparing for the *Sing Along with Mitch* television show. Sometimes, I took Jewish or Methodist friends there just to scare the shit out of them. They went one time and never returned.

As with most Catholic churches, just as you enter the vestibule (lobby), you come upon what I first thought was a water fountain. Hey, I was a little kid and it looked like the one in the backyard; I didn't know. But it turned out to be a figurine font where the Holy Water was kept. You dipped your fingers in it, made the Sign of the Cross and I guess the weekly forgiveness process began. To me, it was a bacteria-sharing and acquisition device. But, I get the symbolism. Still, all those hands in one basin of water.

After exposing myself to hundreds of other people's germs, I then had to find a place to sit down. I walked down a long aisle and tried to find one of the hard, wooden seats to sit on, always looking for a row that did not have old ladies, people coughing, or drunks from the night before already sitting or sleeping there. I would try to find some friends, but they were usually with their parents or just didn't show up that day.

I would sit and wait for what seemed like eternity. The priest would finally enter, and everyone stood up as if the President of the United States had just walked in. Who the heck was this guy to command such acclaim? He said "hi" to everyone, we say "hi" back and the mass would begin, or should I say *The Jack LaLanne Show* was about to begin. (*The Jack LaLanne Show* was a television series about fitness and exercise that ran from 1953 until 1985. This guy was in the greatest shape of anyone you've ever seen. He once pulled a rowboat with a lady in it while swimming across the English Channel—with his teeth!)

Well, the Sunday Catholic church version of the show was about to start. Like I said, it began with everyone having to stand up. After the greetings, he said a few words and we sat down again on the hard wooden seat. After a few more minutes, we stood up again for some other reason. Then we kneeled on this skinny wooden structure on the floor (at least it had a little cushion), and then after more Latin words, we stood back up, then sat again, kneeled again, and sat back down. This madness went on for an hour. Over and over again, you stand, sit, and kneel. It's enough to make your head spin.

Some people even get up to go for short walk to get a cookie and a drink. At least they got to stretch their legs a little. I know I'm just making fun at the whole thing, but c'mon, I was ten years old. Soon I would get my chance to walk around the church and get a cookie, but I had to pass a series of tests first.

I thought the mass was harder on the older folks. Many of them just sat there and smiled during most of the calisthenics. No exercising for them today. Others tried to keep up with the routine but would mess up and made mistakes. When they were supposed to kneel, they started to sit. When they were supposed to sit, they started to kneel. These people looked awkward and drew attention from the seasoned professionals who snickered at them like the good Catholics they were. Others tried to fake it by using the half sit, half kneel move. Oops, didn't mean to sit, I know what to do. Others mumbled the wrong response words to the mass or did not know the words to the songs. I think lip-synching may have been invented at a Catholic mass.

And, to put the final hypocritical topping of whipped bullshit on this one-hour of kid hell, you would see people raising an eyebrow to the awkwardly acting people. You knew just what they were thinking: "Who are these people who only come to church once in a while and have obviously not memorized the important recitals and routines?" To me, it was not how people should think of one another and not a way to waste a Sunday morning better served on the baseball field.

I was a rebellious young lad to say the least, especially when it came to religion. I constantly argued with the nuns, the pastor, or anyone else who tried to shove what I had deemed nonsense down my throat.

I do believe in a higher force, a creator, or whatever you want to call it. I believe it's important to have faith in humanity and to be as good a person as you can be. But I do question stories from the Bible and I wondered why I could not talk in church without getting hit by the nuns in God's house. I wondered why your sins could be easily forgiven on any given Sunday by just going into a wooden shed and telling some guy dressed in black that you were sorry for the bad things you did that week. "I'm so sorry, please forgive me. I promise, I'll never do it again." What a crock!

And I wondered about The Ten Commandments, too. My sister was a nun, okay, so I got more than enough of the Bible and these so-called laws. Always the inquisitive sort, I would ask her, "So, let me get this straight, you do these ten things and that's it, Heaven and eternal joy is within your grasp?" Sounds like a good deal, huh? I don't think so. I know full well I did more than ten categorical things wrong every day, let alone every week when I was a kid. I was of the opinion there should be at least several hundred commandments to fit the ills of modern society, let alone what little kids did wrong. Shit, politicians do at least fifty things wrong each week. Lying, cheating, and stealing are by design, qualifications for any political résumé.

Next, let's discuss the confession box. Remember now, this is the Catholic faith, perhaps the all-time home run leader in man-made laws. That is what it was called, *a confession box*. Yes, it was a box of sort, a small wooden structure inside the church with a revolving door for sinners. Go in a bad person, spill your guts to the priest, and come out a repenting soul with a fresh new start to the week.

The box, as I refer to it, was strategically positioned at the back of the church so the sinners would not gain full access inside the main church until they confessed their sins. It's kind of like going through security at the airport, the Catholic version of the TSA so to speak.

They should have just put in a login pad with a reset button with each person's own code number on the front door of the confession box because we always saw the same people going in and out every week. It was like a membership. How many bad things can one person do in a short period of time to warrant going into the box every week spilling the beans to some guy behind a black curtain? Then again, I guess it was neat being Catholic. You could reshuffle the deck each week and start all over again with a new hand.

I never did grasp the concept of redemption, as I kept doing the same bad things week after week. They should have given rain checks. I did confess when I was sorry for some of the things I did, but I'd already told my sins to God in person. I would kneel at the foot of my bed, put my hands together, and prayed to what I thought was God. Maybe I was sorry for whatever bad things I may have said or done, I don't know for sure. But what I do know, I just kept doing them over and over again.

I would have earned a lot of Marriott miles at that confession booth. I did not do *really* bad things, but rather thirty Hail Mary kind of stuff. Believe me, when I was younger, I was always talking to God. It was my own guilt trip thrust upon me by the politico of a Catholic family. Boy, I'm hammering religion here, but hey it is always ripe for debate and let's face it, it is the core of most conflict in the world.

Now I can't let the priests get off without a few observations. As I mentioned, I had a brother-in-law who had been a priest. Long story, but my sister and he had to get approval from Pope John in Rome to get married so as not to be excommunicated from the Catholic Church. Some faith, huh? Two people fall in love and are required to ask some guy in Italy if it is okay to get married so they will not be banished from your little club. Today, there are women who have been tortured and beaten by their husbands who cannot receive communion if they get divorced.

There has been a lot said and inferred about Catholic priests. But for the most part, the ones I knew were always nice to me. They did have some strange duties and I often questioned why they did such things during the services. For certain masses, especially around the holy days, they would perform strange rituals (and people thought the Indians were crazy for all the weird things they did: dancing, chanting, and smoking whatever in their pipes). I remember this one thing the Catholic priest did, I call it *the smoking can show*.

The priest would light the inside of this lantern-like can on fire and it would start to smoke. It was a kind of incense and I get it that it was symbolic, but still, I was ten years old and this is something I did not understand. He would walk up and down the center aisle of the church waving this smoking can so that the smoke would disperse the incense all around. It turned the whole place into a smog of smelly smoke, sort of like Gotham City. People would start coughing and the kids would be holding their noses because it did not smell so good. Someone should test the long-term side effects on people due to the smoking can. We know second-hand smoke is not good for you.

Well, after the smoking can, the priest goes back to his little box at the alter and gets another object. It was like a larger metal baby rattle with holes it. I think they put holy water inside it and he would walk the aisles showering the people with the holy water filled baby rattle. He would utter a few phrases in Latin that nobody understood and he would try to sprinkle as many people as he could with the baby rattle water. I would see people leaning out of their seats to get a little of the sprinkle of holy water on them. I guess they thought this would help cleanse them of the bad things they did that week. If they did not get sprinkled enough, then it was back to the box.

The concept of donating money for supposed charitable purposes had to have been invented by the Catholic Church. In a strategy to get money into their coffers, who better to hit up than the people who worshipped at the church. What a set up! The donors come to you. This was the first Super Pac. Once the mass started, they even had guys who would go around with baskets on long handles to collect money from the parishioners. We called these guys the tax collectors. The tax collectors would go to all the pews and shove this basket in front of every single person, and not just once during the mass but twice—or even three times during special holidays. A little tricycle bell would ring and the tax collectors would scurry out from their hiding spots to begin their money collecting duties. They came out of the shadows like vampires.

Sometimes people got to see how much money others were giving. The big spenders would donate dollar bills and look around with a weird smile on their face. I guess they thought the more they gave, the better their chances were of getting into Heaven. Some people had little envelopes with their names printed on them and those couldn't be seen through. They even had to buy these envelopes! If someone did not have an envelope and the tax collector shoved the money basket in front of them as it was passed around, everybody could see what they'd given. I remember many a snicker from those people who thought another person was being cheap. If the person had the envelope, nobody knew what they'd given. It could have been empty for all we knew. Imagine the look on the face of the tax collectors opening those empty envelopes.

I think they should have just provided a debit or credit card for weekly donations. They could have called it *Vatican One* with a picture of the Pope on it. He could go on TV and ask, "What's in your wallet?"

Lucky for us kids, nothing much was expected. We always threw in a nickel or some small change and that was good enough. But it was the adults who were put on the spot and subject to the Monday morning news reporting of the Old Ladies Broadcasting Network, station OLBN. "Did you see Mr. Jones in church on Sunday? He was rather stingy this week, blah, blah, blah."

Oh, well, I guess going to church may have done some good.

The Antenna House

CHAPTER 15

Dad, the Uncles, and the TV Antenna

I think it was 1965 when we got our first brand new, *used* color TV set. I don't think many kids today would understand what a used item of anything is. Imagine, using something someone else had discarded or sold because it was old or broken. Anyway, it was an RCA television and it had a 24-inch screen inside an oak cabinet. To me, it was beautiful. It was a little scratched and had a burn mark from where someone left a cigarette burning on the top of it. That did not matter and soon there would be more cigarette burn marks and scratches, but, hey, that's what gave it a little character. It was exciting to finally have a color TV and soon we would be watching our Westerns in red blood and guts color.

Dad brought the TV home one Saturday morning in May, wanting to watch the baseball game on NBC coming up that afternoon. It was being televised in color and you can just imagine a kid's excitement to finally be able to watch the Yankees and Red Sox in full living color. These teams were fierce rivals and to be able to see the grimaces of red faces and the anger of fiery eyes in full color was going to be amazing.

The blue Yankees caps with their pinstriped uniforms contrasting the Red Sox white uniforms with red emblems and team trademark—it was going to be great. These colorful uniforms and the brown chalked-striped infield and green outfield would soon come to life right there in our living room. This was going to be such a huge event that dad invited my Uncle Frankie and Charlie over to watch the game. Plus he had invited half the neighborhood and had several cases of beer chilling in ice coolers for the occasion.

There was one problem, though. Back in those days, there was no cable TV or easy installation software via the Internet. Back then you needed a large TV antenna positioned just so in the right spot high up on the roof to receive the best TV signal. The bigger the antenna, the better, so my dad bought the biggest one he could find.

That brings me to problem number two. We lived in an old two-story Victorian-style house. It was over a hundred years old and had a third story attic where the ghosts lived. So, the roof was like thirty feet high. This would have presented a challenge to even the most skilled TV antenna installers, which these guys were not.

Naturally, problem number three was dad, Uncle Charlie, and Uncle Frankie. They were strong guys, bulls really, but I had a bad feeling about this one.

Well, now it was time to take to task and put this antenna up on the roof. The three rocket scientists decided they would install it up on the roof themselves and nothing was going to stop them. Who needed a professional TV antenna installer when you have over twenty-five years of combined schooling working for you? Remember, all three of these guys were in their forties. Do the math; it's not pretty.

To start with, they steal—I mean borrow—a tall wooden painter's ladder, got plenty of connection wire, and laid out their plans over a few brews. They then mustered the guts to drag the big antenna up the ladder and onto the thirty-foot-high roof to try to attach it to something at the top. The TV antenna was not light, and was about eight feet high and at least six feet across, with two or three sections of various length aluminum rods sticking out. The opening act over, the real show was about to begin, and I'm not talking about the one on the new used TV.

Ever since I can remember, I've had my own personal version of *The Three Stooges*, these guys being the stars of so many comic capers, bungled projects, and memories to, well, write a book about. Over the years of my youth, they provided laughter, disappointment, embarrassment, and numerous lessons, both good and bad. And on this day, they would not let me down. On this day, I laughed during the project, cried a little when they yelled at me, and then smiled at the outcome.

Bolstered with Anheuser courage and beaming in the confidence of their combined skills, they commenced with the installation. Everything appeared to be going well in the initial stages of the project. Using ropes and pulleys, looking like skilled circus acrobats, they somehow managed to get the huge antenna up the ladder and onto the rooftop without damage to the house or themselves. Everything was going nicely and to plan. No one fell off the roof or the ladder, the antenna was not damaged, and it appeared they were on their way to a successful installation.

Up until this point, there was even a very minimal amount of yelling and cursing; rather unusual as yelling and cursing was the norm whenever these guys did anything together. The success or failure of a project involving these guys could easily be gauged by the number of curse words we heard. As the number increased, so would the yelling.

It didn't last and such was the increase in the level of cursing that day, if they had been church-going men and would have had to attend services the next day, they all would have spent a lot of time in the sinner's box. They would be asking forgiveness for taking The Lord's, each other's, and Sears and Roebuck's name in vain. It was a good thing there wasn't any lightning that day because I think God would have lit those three up like a Christmas tree!

Anyway, miracles do happen and they finally got the antenna in place without any major incident. The wires had already been hooked up to the TV, even providing enough slack just in case anything did happen. That was a good idea. I'd seen this show before, and I was glad they wanted to be safe and not have the TV catapulted out of the second-floor window.

Once everything was hooked up, it was my job to monitor the TV for the best possible picture on Channel 10. This was a fixed-positioned antenna, no remote turning to a specific position. It was funny to watch as the TV picture came in very clear when they turned it one way, and then totally fuzzy when it was turned in a different direction. On this day, only Channel 10 mattered and they wanted the very best picture for the game. So, they found the right position and I yelled out of the window, "that is perfect, the channel is coming in clear and with beautiful colors!"

I was so excited. I ran to the kitchen and popped open a Coke, got the chips, and knew that soon, very soon, we would be watching the Yankees and the Red Sox in living color! I knew Dad and the uncles were putting the finishing touches to their marvelous installation and all appeared to be fine and dandy.

But just then—like most everything else these guys got involved in—things took a turn to the unexpected and the real excitement was about to begin. The first sign of trouble was my dad's voice and a few choice curse words, followed by two or three red chimney bricks falling past the window where I was stationed on the second floor.

The bricks had come from the hundred-year-old chimney to which Mo, Larry, and Curley had affixed the antenna. Those bricks were followed by more bricks ... and tools, roof tiles, wires, and ultimately the TV antenna itself. I was like Dorothy in the *Wizard of OZ* looking out of her bedroom window, watching all those crazy things fly past her during the twister. Fortunately, none of the guys fell from the roof.

What happened next was amazing. The antenna spiraled down thirty feet from the roof, and like a missile, crashed back to earth, plunging upside down into the ground. There had been a lot of rain that spring and the ground was very soft, so the antenna stuck into the ground at an odd angle. A few pieces were broken and wires were tangled and flapping all over.

I ran down the stairs, relieved to find dad and the uncles safe on the ground, yelling and blaming one another for what had happened. After a while, we all went back upstairs to calm down. We walked into the living room and lo and behold, the most perfect picture any TV could hope to deliver was there right before our eyes. No one said a word. We got our drinks, ate our popcorn and hot dogs, and sat down to enjoy our first Yankees Red Sox baseball game—in brilliant clarity and full living color.

The antenna, bricks, roof tiles, and even the tools that had fallen off the roof stayed on the lawn for many days, left in the very position as they had been on that fateful day. I think dad was superstitious and that this was a sign from God. Channel 10 came in great for weeks until God reminded us of His power by unleashing a fierce New England storm that blew everything around the yard—and we lost the picture.

We never regained the exceptional picture attained from the expert installation, so it was back to "rabbit ears" and tin foil. Some of you will know what I'm talking about.

Chapter 16

More Ghost Stories

The Ghosts of Chestnut Hill

The Chestnut Street Meeting House, a white, clapboard sided, two-story building located at the corner of Chestnut Hill Road and Thayer Street, was built in the late 1760s. It is located right next to Chestnut Hill Cemetery where the remains of local citizens dating from as far back as 1761 are interred. Some of those, if tales be true, were put there by the local Indian tribe during a brief uprising when they reportedly hacked, scalped, and butchered a good number of the local citizens. The Indians deemed them trespassers and spoilers of their sacred ground.

I don't know where these stories started, but they were handed down through generations of local storytellers. Everyone in town had heard the stories of the rampaging Chestnut Hill Indians back during the colonial period wreaking havoc amongst the locals. Stories of Indian ghosts with tomahawks flying and axes beheading the poor settlers abounded.

The big guys were all too ready to scare the living daylights out of us little guys with these tales. And in typical big guy fashion, they concocted a plan to get some of us to go up to the cemetery one night to meet a challenge from the guys across the tracks on the other side of town.

You see, the town was almost evenly split right down the middle, separated by the railroad tracks. It was like two completely different towns. I think the guys from across the tracks might have been a little tougher than we were because they were always looking for a fight and generally trying to bully us in school and around town. We held our own most of the time, however, and seemed to always beat them in sports.

Anyway, some of the big guys got the across-the-tracks guys to start teasing us and challenged us to a campout at the old Chestnut Hill Cemetery. Whoever could camp out and stay the whole night would go down as being the tougher guys—for a while, at least—and earn respect. Unbeknownst to us, there was a devious plan and collaboration between the big guys and those guys from across the tracks.

It was October, almost Halloween, of course, and it was a full moon to boot. We all agreed it would be Saturday night, with five of our guys and five from their crew. An October night in New England, coupled with sleeping in an old cemetery, was scary enough. Throw in a good story of Indian bloodshed right before going up to the campsite and you've got the makings for high anxiety.

Listening to an old Indian story was part of the deal, so we all had to listen to the tale about the Indian massacre before heading out. The big guys even got some old codger in town to recount the tale at dusk, right before we headed up to the cemetery.

Old Dean Johnson was a town legend and he liked to sip grandpa's cough medicine a bit. But he knew everything about the town history and folklore. He must have told this story a hundred times, scaring the pants off a lot of kids. His face was worn, badly wrinkled, and his clothes weren't always the cleanest. As he told the story, he would take a few swigs out of a bottle in a brown paper bag and would wipe his lips with his fingers. I don't remember drinking soda out of a bag, so it must have been something else.

His storytelling skills were very good and he kept us on edge right up until the climatic, frightful ending, complete with hooting and hollering while pulling out a rubber tomahawk.

As could be expected, the tale did not end well for the town folk. When he was done telling the story, we walked away, quietly trying hard not to show how scared we were. But I'm sure we all had the same visions of screaming, headless Puritans. This memory would last well into the night.

Following Old Dean's story, the two little gangs headed out for the three-mile walk up to Chestnut Hill and the cemetery. The long and narrow street was dark, with only a telephone pole light or distant house light every so often. The ten of us felt fine being together and we were brave enough as a group. But had it just been me alone or with just one other guy, we would have been plenty scared after listening to that story.

There were no cars out that night, only a few houses at the end of long driveways and the greyness of the moonlight in early evening. A dog would howl in the distance and there were the strange noises on the roadside coming from the dark woods. They were probably only little critters prowling around for food—but it also could have been a bloodthirsty Indian out for a night of hatchet hacking.

It took us about an hour to reach the Chestnut Hill Meeting House and the cemetery. The sun had set and except for the light from the full moon, it was totally dark. Our small flashlights flickered like little beacons in the night. We were about to enter the cemetery to fulfill the first part of the dare.

We pushed on the old metal gate and it swung open slowly, squeaking as if it needed a gallon of 3-in-one oil. We passed grave marker after grave marker. The gravestones were weather beaten marble with black and gray streaks running crookedly down the front of the marker, blurring the inscriptions. The combination of two hundred years of weather and the fading white marble turned the headstone facings into an eerie sight. If you stared at these gravestones long enough, you would start to see images of people with contorted horrified faces. Were these the early settlers killed by the bloodthirsty Indians long ago? Were they warning us to turn around and run home?

Once inside the cemetery, the second and final part of the challenge was for the two gangs to split up, each setting up a small camp, and remaining in the cemetery until morning. Of course, the other gang was in cahoots with the big guys, but my guys and I were about to experience the fright of our young lives.

The night started calmly enough. We were still thinking about Old Dean's story, keeping our guard up, but as the first hour passed and nothing happened, our fear subsided a bit and our confidence gained. We bravely told each other, "Indians killing townsfolk and chopping off their heads, what a crock of shit."

We made a little campfire and put hotdogs on sticks to cook them. Then we flamed some marshmallows and shared hot chocolate. We started talking about things other than maniac Indian ghosts. It was getting cold so we got inside the tents, into our sleeping bags, and tried to go to sleep. All we wanted to do was wake up alive and walk into town, expecting the honors of having beaten the dare.

When I zipped the front meshing of the tent, everything was very quiet and so dark. Suddenly, there it was! There was a sound coming from deep in the woods. It couldn't have been our rival gang for they were only about fifty yards away. The sound, distant at first, got louder and we knew something was approaching our camp. It was a screaming sound, as if someone was being chased. It was getting closer and closer. Then the roof of our tent began being hit by small objects.

Our hearts were pounding. I poked my head out of the zippered front of the tent and there, in full headdress and war paint, was an eight-foot-tall Indian. In one hand, he held the bloodied head of a Puritan and in the other the bloodied hatchet with which the head had been severed.

We all screamed in fear and bolted out of our tents, trying to reach the cemetery gate before this crazy Indian got us—but the gate was blocked by another Indian. This one was at least ten feet tall and he had a huge ax. He chased us past the gravestones and out of the cemetery. We ran very fast and soon we were back on the main road heading back to town.

We were huffing and puffing from exhaustion and the most frightful experience we'd ever had. We'd left our camp gear at the unholy site. Still shaking in our stocking feet and wearing only our underwear shorts and t-shirts, we made our way back to our homes and snuck into our beds. I know I didn't get to sleep that night.

In the morning, we all met at the candy store and sure enough, we found three of the more notorious big guys sitting on the fence, laughing as we approached, and drinking sodas with our rival gang members.

Our rivals asked us if we'd slept well the night before. One of them said, "it was so peaceful there in the cemetery last night, I slept like a baby." The three big guys started whooping like Indians and raising their hands as if they were crazy maniacs.

Realizing the scam, we felt humiliated. We were victims of a big joke and one that would forever live in the annuals of the town's version of the kids' History Channel.

For a long time after, even the adults would mock us with Indian jokes and gestures of hand-chopping hatchets. The hand-chopping tomahawk ritual was developed that year in our little town, not by the Atlanta Braves baseball fans in the 1990s.

Ghosts in the Woods

You can tell by now *the Woods* was a special place for me and my friends. It was somewhere we could go and be free from parents, schoolteachers, and well, adults in general. Heck, no adult could even follow us through the paths and trails we blazed in this forest of our youth.

There were several key meeting spots in the woods and they each had a name. They had to have a name. How else would we have known where to meet? The Big Rock was a huge piece of granite sticking out of the earth on top of one the hills. Cranberry was a pond where we skinny-dipped in the summer and skated in the winter. The Fort, the Old Sod House, and other kid-coined landmarks were places where we met up, played, and camped out.

We built tree houses and made snow sled runs during the winter. We did all of this without any parental supervision. We got our fair share of bruises, sprained ankles, and cuts working on these precarious projects, but nobody ever got seriously injured. Parents half expected the minor scrapes we came home with. My mom used to say, "looks like somebody had fun today."

There was one time when this kid got sprayed by a skunk we had been chasing. As he was trying to run away from the skunk, he fell into a swampy area and got covered in mud, and yes, he smelled horrible. Sometimes an unlucky event like this results in a nickname for life. From that day on, we called this poor kid Stinky Swamp Rat. Sometimes we just called him Swamp Rat or plain ol' Stinky. Turned out that good old Stinky Swamp Rat ended up becoming a local politician. Go figure. Sometimes fate just unfolds in a natural order, or should I say odor.

The woods were beautiful and mysterious, although at night, they could be scary and dangerous. When it got dark in the woods, it seemed like all kinds of strange sounds came out and were amplified in the warm New England summer air. Strange insects, birds, and critters would sing their night songs. It was even scarier if you'd watched a vampire movie recently. As you know, vampires always come out at night and we knew the woods were full of them. When you are young, the nightly sounds in the woods take on a different tone and your mind races with visions of creepy things.

Sometimes, while camping outside in the woods, it would start to rain so hard that small rivers would form right outside the tent. We would be trapped inside and could only hope the rain would not get inside the tent and drown us. Boy, we could have used that submarine. But the hard rain pounding on the canvas of the tent was also like a sleeping pill. The sound of the rain soon became soothing, lulling us to sleep. In the morning after a hard rain, there was nothing like the clean, fresh smell in the air when waking in the woods. Allergy kid never wheezed or sneezed when waking up there after a good rain.

Naturally, there were also ghosts in the woods. Ghosts were everywhere in New England. There was the lost skater from Cranberry Pond, the old settler who died in the sod house, and the maniac drivers of the deserted old junk cars. These were just a few of the spirits that haunted the woods.

Cranberry Pond was about a mile or so from the back of my house. In the winter, it froze over with ice thick enough to ice skate on. Legend went that a kid fell thought the ice and drowned in the icy water one winter. He was never found, but each spring an old toke (hat), a mitten, or a scarf would be found frozen, visible in the thinning top layer of the ice. The articles stayed frozen there all winter, a ghastly reminder of the body somewhere below in the pond that was certainly by now a zombie.

We later found out that each winter one of the big guys would hike out there and plant a few items in the water early in winter right before the pond would freeze. That would cement the story for the coming season and ensure that the little guys would not stay out there too late. Maybe they were trying to protect us. Time passed and we took over as the big guys. I remember going to Cranberry Pond in early winter and playing the same ruse for a new group of little guys. Some things never change.

The Old Sod House was, well, we weren't sure what it was. It was old and made from earth dug out and shaped into squares that fit together. There was an unusually large sunken section of the ground close by where the builders must have dug out the dirt to use to make the earthen squares. A good part of the sides remained and it looked like it could have been a small room many years ago. It wasn't large but there were Indians in these woods at one time and maybe it was something they had used. Or just maybe the Indians had killed the old guy who lived there.

We used to dig all around this area and found lots of old cans, utensils, and bottles. I even found an 1863 Indian Head one-cent piece there—which I still have. I don't know where it started, but legend had it that the house was haunted with the spirit of an old man who had lived there. Every so often we would go there just before nightfall, usually on a dare, and hang out for a while to see if there was any truth to the legend. There were critters mulling around inside the sod house and they made enough strange noises to convince us there was indeed a ghost inside. Never could prove it... but never could disprove it, either. Best keep those spirits undisturbed.

There was another place in the woods, an open field where three or four old cars had been left abandoned. These were cars from the late 1940s that had been bashed, looted for whatever usable parts they may have had, and then left to be used for rock throwing practice. When not pelting these old cars with stones, we would crawl inside and sit behind what was left of the steering wheel and pretend to be racing around the track smashing into other cars.

The cars all had names, but I can only remember two of them. The Great Pumpkin was an old orange Chevy and The Green Crapper was a big old-fashioned car from way back that we didn't even know the make or model of. The seats of these old cars were filthy and had broken glass everywhere, and at times, the remains of a dead animal was sitting on the seat next to us. No matter, we'd take him for a ride, too.

One time the big guys, always wanting to scare the living daylights out of us, planted a skeleton inside one of the cars. It was one of those plastic skeletons from a high school science lab, but from a distance, it looked like the real thing.

One afternoon, they somehow knew we were heading over to the junk car area. The closer we got to the open field where the cars were, the more clearly we could see this strange figure behind the wheel of The Green Crapper. Atop his skull head he wore a black derby hat, along with dark sunglasses and a green necktie around his skeleton neck. His bony hands were glued to the wheel and a cigarette was hanging out of the side of his mouth.

As we got closer to the car, we could see more of the ghastly figure. We were startled by the sound of crashing metal and broken glass when suddenly the maniac skeleton driver twitched!

Our eyes locked on this twitching maniac skeleton driver and we froze in our tracks. We were about forty yards from the cars when another round of crashing metal and broken glass started! The skeleton was still twitching and then we heard weird laughter. We knew we had to get out of there quickly before the maniac driver came at us. We ran home as fast as we could, finally arriving at my porch panting and gasping for air. We never told anybody about this. Who would have believed us?

We later found out that the big guys had planted the skeleton and several of them hid behind the cars using tire irons to bang on the side of the cars, smash windows, and tail and headlights. One of guys had ropes tied to the skeleton to make him move. It was real low-end horror film stuff. But remember, we were only ten years old and we still believed in werewolves, Dracula, and zombies. This maniac skeleton driver was very real to us.

I don't know how these guys always knew where we were going or what we were doing, but they did and used it to their advantage to terrorize us. Most of my friends had a big brother, so I guess one of the rats was amongst them.

And that was the legend of The Maniac Demolition Derby Driver!

The Quonset Hut

The Quonset Hut was also in the woods. It was another old abandoned structure that you would not have let little kids go exploring in, right? The Quonset Hut was an aluminum framed house that was a long, narrow structure with a continuous rounded roof. It looked like an old space station or an army barracks. But, what was it doing way out there in the woods by itself? My dad said it was used by the government to spy on the Russians during the 1950s. Okay, that sounds about right, dad, the FBI and U.S. Intelligence holed up in Millville, camping out in a crappy aluminum hut spying on Khrushchev. Oh, well, who's to argue with an adult?

The hut had been raided many times by generations of kids. We would see hobos coming out of it every once in while, so it did provide an overnight shelter for a few transients. But it was filthy in there and included the remains of an odd assortment of dead animals. There's nothing like the carcass of a decomposing possum to brighten your day.

Electricity once powered the place and there were lots of wires coming out of the ceiling and walls, just sticking out here and there. Broken glass was everywhere and there was an assortment of junk to pick through, enough to keep a kid busy for a few hours. We would spend hours looking at old yellowed newspapers, old photographs of weird looking people in cracked frames, and shattered housewares from long ago.

The Quonset Hut was not haunted. It was too crappy even for a ghost to hang out in. It was just a place to explore every so often just to let one's imagination run wild. It was a little dangerous, but then again, wasn't everything we did back then?

More Ghosts

It seems we never got enough of the spirit world. A cold draft, an eerie fog, or a foul stench could conjure up images of ghouls and fiends. Throw in the fact that it was Halloween night and you can imagine what runs through a kid's mind. Now, I must have crossed the street in front of my house at night a thousand times before. It was a simple two lane road, not many cars, and almost always very quiet. But on Halloween night, the shadows from the branches of the trees dancing on the pavement looked like a hundred black snakes squirming their way to bite me.

Each whisper of wind played through the streetlight, guiding tree branches on their devilish shadow dance before me.

On that night, I ran as fast as I could to Eddie's house. I stumbled and dropped my flashlight but left it behind, as surely the black snakes would have gotten me had I gone back to get it. I would get another flashlight at Eddie's house.

The next stop was to go with my friend and venture up the dirt road across from his house to meet up with a few other friends with whom we would go trick-or-treating. The dirt road was only a half-mile or so, but it was dark and not without a story or two of some grisly affair that happened along its trail. Here was where the Fog Monster lurked. This creature would suddenly appear out of nowhere to confuse the dirt road traveler and lead him into the dark wooded area near a stream where the traveler would often fall prey to the Fog Monster's henchmen.

Fog and dense mists often rose over these old New England stream-side dirt roads, fog so thick that at times you could lose your way and wander into the woods and plunder into the small brook that ran along the road. You could fall in the brook, scrape your knee, and get full of mud. A tree branch would scrape your face or you would run into the prickly briar to add a few more scratches. Nasty stuff that prickly briar.

One Halloween night I looked so frightful from all the damage the Fog Monster had laid upon me that I did not even dress up for the event. I went trick or treating as I was, already scratched, bloodied, bandaged, and as harried as a hobo. Everywhere we went, people told me I had the best costume. Hey, I lived in dangerous times.

CHAPTER 17

Youth Employment

My First and Worst Job— Material Handler First Class

I think everyone remembers his or her very first paying job. We also remember the absolute worst job we ever had. Well, both of those memorable events happened to me when I was fourteen years old.

I was sweet on a farmer's daughter and she lived on, well, a farm. Let's call this farmer's daughter, Mary. Her father had cows, pigs, and chickens, the whole deal. The cows were kept in a big barn and there was always plenty of work to do taking care of the animals and the day-to-day chores around the farm.

One day, Mary arranged for me to talk with her father about getting a part-time job at the farm after school. I think she liked me and wanted me to be around. I met her dad, a big burly guy dressed in farmer jeans and a baseball cap that had a picture of a tractor on it.

He told me he had a position open for a material handler. I thought, *yes, material handler; sounds important!* The job paid $1.50 per hour. I envisioned that soon I would be driving a tractor or some big farm machine bailing up cut fields of grass into hay bales. Mary would surely think I was so cool driving the tractor.

Well, no such luck. Who is going to trust a fourteen-year-old kid with expensive farm equipment? As it turned out, material handlers worked only in the barn and started at four o'clock every afternoon. Seems that this was just about the time that all the cows were coming back to the barn from the pastures after a full day of doing nothing but eating all the grass they could consume while in the field. Getting the picture yet?

The cows were herded into their stalls in the barn. They entered the stalls with their heads facing away from the barn's main alley, which goes right down the middle of the barn. The other end of the cow, well, it was positioned so that any *material* that came out fell into a long trough that ran the entire length of the barn. And the barn was *very* long. The material handler's job was to use a long pole with a big metal square at the end that fit precisely into the trough and starting at one end of the barn, push the "material" the entire length of the trough, down to an area where it was collected and then mixed with hay to create fertilizer that was then pumped into the silos.

I lasted about one hour doing this horrible task. The final straw was after I had pushed the material all the way down the trough for a second time and I looked back and saw that there was now more material in the trough than when I had first started handling it. And the material kept coming faster and faster—only now it included liquid as well as solid material.

Who could do this job? Was there not a machine or some automated system to do it? It was insane. I threw down my high-tech equipment, took off the large pair of rubber boots the boss had given me and ran out of the place as fast as I could. I did not even want the $1.50 that I was entitled to for the one hour of torture I had experienced. I would have paid $1.50 to leave the place.

I soon forgot about Mary, but I have dreaded farms and especially cows ever since. Cows scare me like clowns do little kids. Farm cows are not like the nice clean ones you see on TV, in a painting, or from afar in a field. They are mostly always dirty, smell bad, and manufacture a lot of material. It took a long time for me to get rid of the foul odor in my nose and forget the awful sights of that day.

Yes, I will forever remember my first paying job as Material Handler.

Football Cards and Uncle Frankie

I was introduced to the world of gambling and hustling at a young age. In 1967, the National Football League was expanded to sixteen teams. My Uncle Frankie was a shady character to start with—one day he was driving a Cadillac and handing out money and the next he is walking and broke. But still, he was my favorite uncle and he was always looking out for me. So, he came to me one day during football season and gave me twenty of these football cards with the names of all the NFL teams on it.

The cards are used to bet $1.00 on picking all sixteen winning teams that week. If you guessed all sixteen, you won a lot of money. If you picked fifteen out of sixteen winning teams, you won less money, and so on. But it was nearly impossible for anyone to win much more than a few dollars.

The only catch was if someone did win, we would have to pay them. Oh, there were a few lucky ones down through the years and when that happened, my Uncle Frankie was looking at losing a good chunk of change. But we usually came out way ahead.

My foray to the dark side started with me peddling a few of

these cards here and there to my friends. My uncle would give me $.25 for each card I sold. Not bad for a little kid. It was easy at first and I had my group of regular buddies that every week would try their luck. Then other people around town found out I was selling these cards. Soon, I was selling a hundred cards and then two hundred every week. I was earning thirty, forty sometimes up to fifty dollars a week during football season when I was only thirteen years old!

Keep in mind, the minimum wage in 1967 was $1.65 per hour and a lot of people did not even bring home forty dollars after taxes. I did not pay taxes and customers came to me for the cards. After a while, everybody in town and in school was buying these cards, including the local police, the guys at the firehouse, schoolteachers, and anyone looking to beat the odds and have a big payday.

Nobody ever won the big prize, though. The odds of getting all sixteen correct, was like one out of 150,000. I would sell a few thousand of the cards each season so I was safe. Every so often, someone would get fifteen out of sixteen and I would have to pay them twenty dollars. Big deal. I had plenty of cash in my savings can from all the other losers. But I wasn't very thrifty back then and spent most of the money on stupid stuff and taking care of my pals.

Nonetheless, it was a good experience for a couple of years and it taught me that easy money, not to say illegal money, was not the real world. I would have to learn to work harder, save better, and respect the people who were trying to do just that. I would learn soon enough that it was going to be hard to a get ahead in the real world.

CHAPTER 18

Danger Everywhere

Now, I know times are different and certainly parents are a lot more protective of their children than they were in my day. And really, they need to be because the world has gotten so out of sorts. It wasn't that my parents cared less than they should have; it's more that we were a lot more self-reliant. We were on our own more and depended upon our friends and neighbors to take an active interest in our lives. There is an ancient proverb, "It Takes a Village to Raise a Child." That was so true in my day where in a small town your neighbors were trusted friends, the shopkeepers were honest businessmen, and your friends were your friends. You had a lot of people looking out for you.

Don't think we did not have our share of weird people, perverts, and even child molesters. These monsters were not invented in just the past twenty years; they have been around forever, hiding in the shadows, always a threat. But back in the day, in our little town and thousands of towns across the USA, this behavior was dealt with swift and severe justice. Millville was not a sanctuary city. We should take a few notes from the past and put a halt to a justice system that protects criminals.

Our parents grew up tough and independent, as did we. Look at all the stories you have just read. By today's measure, my friends and I should all have been severely injured or killed during any one of these escapades. But none were lost. But then again, looking for the Pokémon has proven dangerous.

I doubt any parents today will let their children read this book. It is a glimpse into what once was and what may never be again. History repeats itself and we learn from it, but we will most likely never revisit the days of our youth and the innocence of these times.

The Pussification of America

Yes, there were plenty of scrapes, cuts, and bruises along the way, but heck, I'm still here and many of my old buddies are still kicking, too. Things are different today. Even today's ballplayers, especially the pitchers, are sissified into a culture that harms them. Today's major league pitchers, with their limited pitch count and the endless catering to are being injured at a far greater rate than the guys who pitched entire games many times season after season.

Nolan Ryan, Gaylord Perry, Ferguson Jenkins, Bob Gibson, and a host of others took pride and were expected to pitch the whole game. Today, a hundred pitches or five innings and the guy did a great job. Good job, Joey! You pitched five innings. Joey's done his job and now he is so tired he has to rest for the next five days. Poor Joey. But he gets to collect his fat salary, so don't feel sorry for poor Joey.

Yes, I believe the pussification of America started with the latest generations. That's right, I'm talking about you twenty- and thirty-year-old people of today that my generation raised! Forget the teenagers and youngsters of today; they are doomed to a life of coddling, sippy-cups, safe-zones, and chasing Pokémon. And it's our fault. Most of us, wanting to give more to our kids than we had, helped create the environment we have today. It's not our children's fault. They are merely responding to what you and I have tried to do for them. We should have been tough with them like our parents.

I cringe when I watch youngsters play today, seeing eight- and nine-year-old kids with training wheels on their bikes, receiving trophies and prizes for coming in sixteenth place. I see little kids wearing helmets to protect their coddled little brains, sure, but I also see kids just walking around with helmets on! Prior generations got by without helmets and we produced some of the finest minds. Einstein did okay as did many other inventors, world and business leaders.

Today, I saw two boys shooting baskets. They were at least twelve years old, but were as tall as I am, yet the basket was lowered to about six feet high. Are you kidding me? When I was a kid, the basket was ten feet high, just like it should be. You learned to jump and use two hands on the ball to throw it up there or heave it up to reach the net. Heck, the poles could not even be lowered if we wanted them to be. And most times, the basketball goal was nailed to the front of the garage, so there was no pole to adjust and no lowering of the net so little farts can easily reach it.

The same thing with tee-ball. When did tee-ball happen? I must have missed that meeting. Here little Johnny, see if you can hit this stationary ball placed on a pedestal. My daughter was hitting a soft-toss plastic ball when she was four years old. These little pussies can't even hit the tee-ball! They swing, miss the ball, and knock the stand down! This goes on for hours as the little farts never really learn how to hit a ball.

I know this sounds harsh, and yes there are times when little guys and gals need some help. But, I think kids don't need to be spoon-fed and coddled so much. They need to learn to lose sometimes and that everyone does not always get a trophy. Failure is part of life and disappointment is a reality that needs to be experienced. Everyone fails at one time or another. We should not be rewarding them for every little thing they do.

When they get older, graduate college, and enter the workforce, they will find out that not everyone gets the corner office or the six-figure job without having to earn it. Boys, in particular, will need to toughen up. We have seen the rise of women in business, sports, politics, and a host of professions displacing men. How come? Well, think about it, they had to work harder for it and now they are being rewarded. Wasn't it great to see girls play in the 2014 Little League World Series? One gal was gassing seventy mph fastballs by the boys. Watch out guys, the gals are here and they aren't going away.

Epilog

Reflection

So, there you have it. These stories were recollections of only a few short years in my life. A similar pattern of bizarre adventures with my friends followed through my teens and twenties. If you ask my wife, the pattern continues to this day. Seems one never runs out of stories to tell, or maybe I just have a knack for being in the right place with peculiar people at the wrong time. I hope the generation of today has an opportunity to experience at least a few of the rights of passage I did and will be able to tell a few good stories to their children.

We all have stories about our lives. How we grew up, the friends we made and lost, the places we've been and the crazy things we did. Every person could fill pages with memories and experiences. I'm certain many would be even more interesting, stranger, and funnier than the ones you have just read. So, go ahead, think about your life and your experiences. I'm certain there are people who would want to read about it. Write it down now before it's too late.

Every so often, I go back to Millville, Massachusetts. I see the house I grew up in, the fields where my friends and I played, and even visit a few of the folks who still call it home. I walk the streets strolled so long ago. I will never forget this simple place, my friends, and the memories of my youth.

So, as I sit here in my rented car on Main Street, it is fitting the song *Two Dollar Novels* by Darden Smith is playing on the radio. I turn left off Main Street and through my old neighborhood one more time. Forty years later it still looks and feels the same. Some of the buildings have changed or are not there anymore. Dead Man's Curve was straightened out a long time ago and the old roads have been improved a bit. But a place is not just about buildings and roads. One's old hometown is a feeling, a comfortable easiness. It is a longing for a chance to run through those fields and schoolyards once again. And yes, a great time to reflect on the friends I made and our wild adventures.

I went on to live in this small town until I met the love of my life, married, and raised a family. But these were the early life-forming years and I would not have traded them for a million dollars. Well maybe a million… make that two with inflation.

JOE BARBRIE and his loving wife of 40 years, Christine, live in Northern California. He is a successful entrepreneur and executive in the global medical device industry with over 35 years of experience with small and large companies. Together, Joe and his wife raised two children, Jeff and Jen. Both have gone on to successful careers as healthcare professionals.

www.ingramcontent.com/pod-product-compliance
Lightning Source LLC
Chambersburg PA
CBHW052307300426
44110CB00035B/2169